Tresco Abbey Garden

Mike Nelhams

Annabella,

Very best wishes from Tresco
I hope you enjoyed the garden

Mike Nelhams

TO ISOBEL, MAXINE AND KATIE

TRESCO ABBEY GARDEN

A PERSONAL AND PICTORIAL HISTORY

Mike Nelhams

DYLLANSOW TRURAN

Text © Mike Nelhams 2000
Cover illustration © Jerry Harpur.
Back cover illustration © Derek Harris
Back cover Robert and Lucy Dorrien-Smith with Mike Nelhams © Paul Armiger
Illustrations © the author unless otherwise acknowledged
Photograph of Tresco from the air (Tresco Estate)

ISBN 1 85022 137 5 (cased)
ISBN 1 85022 138 3 (paperback)
A catalogue reference is available from the British Library.

Published by Dyllansow Truran, Croft Prince, Mount Hawke, Truro, Cornwall. TR4 8EE.

Designed by Peter Bennett, St Ives 01736 793170
Printed & bound in Cornwall by R. Booth (Bookbinder) Ltd & Troutbeck Press, Antron Hill, Mabe, Penryn. TR10 9HH

Main text set in Monotype Perpetua and Helvetica Neue Black

THE PHOTOGRAPHS
Paul Armiger
Roy Cooper
Dorrien-Smith family albums
Frank Gibson
Jerry Harpur
Derek Harris
GJ King
Lawry family albums
Andrew Lawson
Alasdair Moore
Simon McBride
Frank Naylor
Tresco Estate
GKN Westland
Fiona Wilding

CONTENTS

THE FAMILY

THE GARDEN

THE PLANTS

ACKNOWLEDGEMENTS

In writing these acknowledgements first and foremost I would like to thank Robert and Lucy Dorrien-Smith for permission not just to write about this extraordinary dynasty, but also to forage about in the family archives and albums with complete freedom.

I gathered from Helen Dorrien-Smith many personal memories of her father Major Arthur, but especially about his plant hunting expeditions and from Teona Dorrien-Smith recollections of island life with her father Commander Tom.

My thanks to Nigel Holman of Chyverton for spending time in recalling past island visits of horticultural interest; to William Waterfield and Carolyn Hanbury, of La Mortola, for inspiration; to Dora Fearnley for unexpectedly appearing at the right moment festooned with notes on her father, head gardener George Andrews.

I am indebted to all Abbey gardeners and students, past and present, for advice, but particularly like to include Peter Clough, Frank Naylor, David Hopkins, Dick Bird, Steve Parkes, Dave Inch, Francis Brint, Ron Gleadle and Alasdair Moore for their past practical contribution to the garden. To Roy Lancaster, Alan Titchmarsh, Chris Brickell, Martyn Rix, Peter Barnes, the Hon. H.E. and Mrs Boscawen, Roy Cheek, Tim Smit, Major Tony Hibbert and Phillip McMillan-Browse for help and encouragement throughout my horticultural career.

A particular handshake is needed to Andrew Lawson who has shared the last fifteen years as we worked together on numerous garden projects, also to Alasdair for unscrambling and making sense of a number of overlong paragraphs, equally to Tony Reading for his willingness to cycle across the island on wet and windy days on a regular basis to rescue lost text from within the bowels of my computer, when I had long since been ready to throw in the towel.

Lastly I would like to thank the publishers Ivan and Heather Corbett. Only through their initial idea, suggestions and constant encouragement has this book made an appearance - with much patience on their part and helpful prodding to keep me going in the right direction. They have steered me through the whole process with enthusiasm and the patience of adults teaching a small child some simple task!

INTRODUCTION

Tresco Abbey Garden is most unusual. The influences that have produced the special and unique qualities of the garden are a diverse mixture of location, climate and fashion, combined with the particular skills and interests of each generation of my family that have left their mark.

Although the garden was started in the 1830s as a small formal area around the newly-built Tresco Abbey, it soon grew in both size and scope. Since that time each garden owner has persued their particular interest within the framework laid down by the previous generations. These interests have included architecture, botany in the scientific sense as well as art and innovation.

Above all the garden is an expression of one family's love of a particular place. It is one of a handful of great gardens still run by the family that created them. Mike Nelhams' book reflects the personal nature of this wonderful place and all the efforts of people, past and present, who have helped to not only preserve the original concept, but to constantly adapt to new ideas.

I hope you enjoy this excellent book.

Right: Lighthouse Walk up to Neptune. (Andrew Lawson)

FOREWORD

To say that Tresco Abbey Garden is special is rather like saying that Darcy Bussell is quite a good dancer, or that Luciano Pavarotti can sing a bit.

Tresco is unique. Its climate, coupled with the vision of one man in the early nineteenth century and the hard work of countless more men and women since, have made it what it is today – a jewel that shines out of the sea just off the toe of England.

I love visiting Tresco, not only because of its dream-like situation (and I have been there in fair weather and foul), but also because of the rich diversity of plants that carpet its shores; plants that you will be hard pressed to find growing so well in any other parts of Britain.

But this is no Shangri-La. When the weather is unkind here it is brutal and, as you'll discover in this book, there are times when nature flexes her muscles and wreaks havoc among Tresco's treasury of plants. All the gardeners can do then is clear up and start all over again – which they have done – with heavy heart and bleeding fingers – on more than one occasion.

That's another reason why I am so fond of the island – the friendliness and good nature of its inhabitants – especially the garden's curator Mike Nelhams. He reckons that he has the best gardening job in the world. I reckon he probably has – after mine!

Here he has told the story of Tresco Abbey Garden as he sees it – from the early days when Augustus Smith first came here, to the present tenure of his current descendants. Then there are Mike's own experiences of developing and tending the garden and its plants. It's a delightful story. I hope when you've read it that you'll feel as fond of Tresco as I do and want to come back again and again. If circumstances keep you away, then try growing the seeds from its Echiums and Furcreas, Puyas and Agapanthus in your own garden.

Oh, I know from bitter experience that some of them will not survive long; but while they thrive you can be reminded of your visit, and when they perish you have the best excuse to come back and look at this wonderful garden again.

Anyway, that's my story and I'm sticking to it.

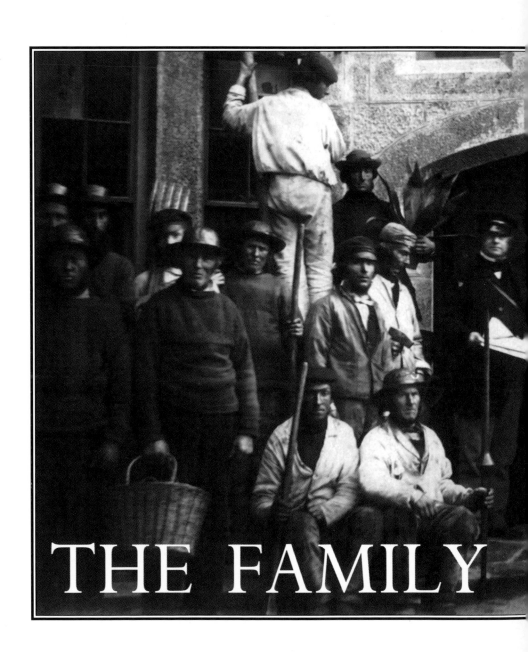

THE FAMILY

Augustus Smith in the Abbey Courtyard with his estate workers. (Robert A. Dorrien-Smith)

14

Right: Augustus
Smith admiring his
Puya chilensis.
(Robert A.
Dorrien-Smith)

AUGUSTUS SMITH

"A young man in need of occupation"

In 1834 a handsome young man of independent means leased all the Isles of Scilly for 99 years or three lifetimes from the Duchy of Cornwall. Although the rent was a nominal £40 a year the Crown imposed a 'fine' of £20,000 and stipulated that £5,000 be spent within six years on improvements. These included a new pier at St Mary's and the completion of the Parish Church. In addition there was the responsibility for the stipends of the local clergy and a solid commitment to revitalise the economy of the off-islands: Tresco, Bryher, St Martin's, St Agnes and at that time Samson. It was unlikely that there would be a return on the capital for many years, if ever. What drove this young man from the comforts of fashionable life and conversation to the deprivations of life on the islands is beyond the scope of this book.

Augustus John Smith was born in 1804, the eldest son of a landed Hertfordshire gentleman. After the benefits of a seemingly conventional education at Harrow and Christ Church, Oxford, Smith returned to the family seat of Ashlyns Hall and immersed himself in the parish affairs of Berkhamstead and Northchurch, particularly education. Smith was single-minded, resolute, determined with indefatigable energy and administrative flair - the position of Lord Proprietor was ideal.

In the early years of the nineteenth century the islands were impoverished and until the arrival of Smith the future looked bleak. His influence, vitality and practical ideas soon created full employment for those that wanted it. His money provided the spark that roused the naturally industrious islanders. The larger ships that were able to come into the new quay brought work for most sections of the community from pilots, shipwrights, dockers and of course farmers ready to send produce for restocking ships or for sale on the mainland. Indeed the 1841 census recorded that sixty-six trades were being followed in the islands. Smith began to build new and better houses for the islanders.

Smith's ideas were based on the utilitarian principles of Jeremy Bentham, whereby work was rewarded and the weak went under. He had four goals: good education for children; to stamp out smuggling; to stop the practice of dividing family holdings and finally to prepare well ordered leases for long term improvement of the land and building stock by the islanders themselves. It is well recorded that his arbitrary style of government did not win Smith a great many friends amongst the generally ungrateful population but his independent character was well able to cope with this. In Hertfordshire he and his views had been denounced from the pulpit on many occasions; controversy was meat and drink to him. One of his greatest triumphs was the introduction of compulsory education on the islands, forty years before this occurred on the mainland. A contribution had to be made by parents of one penny a week per child to attend school. If they did not make regular appearances that week then a fine of two pence was levied. He employed more teachers, increased their salaries and equipped schoolrooms with everything needed for a good all-round education. Smith saw these young children as the long-term future of the islands and he was determined to help them in the right direction. He took an active interest in all individuals. Many older children returned from sea to join the classes seeing the benefits gained from acquiring even the most rudimentary of skills. Smith was proud of the fact that many boys from his schools who went to sea rose to become officers, masters and captains.

A GREAT GARDEN IS BORN

Initially Smith lived on St Mary's, but he quickly appreciated he wanted privacy and space to build in the style and

Above:
Mesembry-anthemum *from South Africa. (Andrew Lawson)*

16

comfort he was used to. His choice of Tresco was not a difficult one. Tresco has a central position and is well protected from the Atlantic Ocean by other islands. In the ninth century the priory of St Nicholas, attached to the Benedictine Tavistock Abbey, was founded and a monastic order survived there until the sixteenth century. Smith surmised that monks always lived in reasonable shelter with a good water supply: Tresco had both. Very little was actually left of the Old Abbey: two archways and some broken down walls on the edge of a hillside at the southern end of the island, protected on the north and west. To the north west of these ruins Smith planned to build his house: the site of the Old Abbey would make the perfect setting for his new garden.

Very little of the island had any vegetation above the height of a gorse bush and the harsh salt gales of the Atlantic Ocean were the prime enemy to any proposed horticultural endeavour, so for his new garden Smith laid out a wall, 3.6m (12ft) high to the west and a little lower to the south, around the ruined priory as protection. It was within these walls that the Abbey Garden began. Incorporated into this design was the "Pebble Garden". Planned in the shape of the Union Jack, it was annually planted with red, white and blue bedding plants. The stones that formed the edging of the borders were collected by the Abbey gardeners who searched in the tidal areas of the beach for many hundreds of matching stones. They collected symmetrical rounded granite pebbles smoothed by centuries of erosion.

This relatively small area gave some formality to his early plantings. He decided to take advantage of the clement Scillonian climate. Warmer than average winters with very few frosts, high light levels and more hours of sunshine in the winter meant that plants would usually grow all the year round. Plants were sent from the Royal Botanic Gardens at Kew and others came from contacts across the world. However it was those plants from South Africa, Australia and New Zealand that proved the most successful. Humidity from the sea and low rainfall figures also contributed to the high proportion of plants from the warmer Mediterranean regions of the world. In later years many of the young Scillonian mariners who Smith had educated returned with seeds, plants and cuttings.

But salt-laden gales were an all-year-round problem. Smith realised very quickly that long-term shelter was needed with mature trees of some size to protect his planned garden. He decided to use the common gorse bush as a 'nurse' plant to shelter his very earliest plantings. The garden had expanded beyond the Old Abbey walls to take in the south facing slopes and surrounding hillsides. Here Smith began his shelterbelt planting. He planted many species of trees and very quickly found two which tolerated the salty gales better than most. From the Monterey Peninsula in California came *Cupressus macrocarpa* and *Pinus radiata* (then known as *Pinus insignis)*; both were fast growing, easy to germinate and evergreen and were in later years to provide the backbone for future plantings. He

Right: One of the earliest photographs of the garden: The Long Walk c1870. (Robert A. Dorrien Smith)

designed the garden to be south facing, protected from salt gales and any icy blasts by the hillsides on the north and west sides.

In his time, as today, the garden had three major walks: the Top Terrace, the Middle Terrace and the Long Walk. All run from east to west; assorted paths join them together, while the lower section of the garden below the Long Walk follows a less structured path with not so much formality. A series of steps was constructed from the top to the bottom of the garden running north to south and at the head and beyond the steps sits an old ship's figurehead from the wreck of the *S.S. Thames* which was placed in position in 1841. Known as the "Neptune Steps" this central staircase has dominated the garden ever since.

At an early stage Smith began to collect figureheads and wreck mementoes which for several years stood on the terrace at the Abbey. Later he built an open fronted building to house the collection. In 1870 he was presented with two tons of large seashells by German sailors whose ships were sheltering in St Mary's Roads. The shells were used to decorate the walls of "Valhalla", as he named his collection, and can still be seen today.

Smith had by this time become a plantsman of some repute and like-minded garden owners such as Lord Ilchester donated many plants from Abbotsbury, on the Dorset coast, which was also able to grow many tender southern hemisphere species. In 1850 Smith made contact with Sir William Hooker, Director of the Royal Botanic Gardens, Kew. Many plants came from Kew to the Abbey Garden over the next three years, enlarging the collection substantially. South African aloes mixed with mesembryathemum and aeonium filled every available rockface and crevice. In the lower areas of the garden a mixture of trees and shrubs from Australia and New Zealand was beginning to gain some height as they fought the southerly gales. By the summer of 1858 Smith had completed his grand design. We know from the letters that he wrote to a close friend, Lady Sophia Tower, that the garden had begun to flourish with a variety of plants not normally able to grow outdoors in the British Isles. Smith began to create areas within the garden that reflected countries across the world: "Australia" had specimens of *Acacia*, *Melaleuca* and *Cassia*; "Mexico" was festooned with *Yucca* and *Furcrea* and "South Africa Flats" full with *Leucadendron*, *Drosanthemum* and *Sparmannia*: all names then not familiar to the British mainland gardener.

In 1866, when Sir William had been succeeded by his son Sir Joseph Hooker as Director of Kew, the plant trafficking between both gardens was re-established with a consignment of Mesembryanthemum cuttings sent to Tresco.

Large quantities of plants then moved between Tresco and Kew on a very regular basis over the next six years. On many occasions plants would arrive as unmarked specimens, simply labelled "Temperate Plants". In this manner the collection exploded into vast numbers and Smith was particularly pleased at the number of species in flower in the winter months. This gave rise to the enthusiastic New Year's Day flower count: an idea which has been taken up subsequently in a number of gardens. It is also recorded that garden visitors began to arrive in quite large numbers in the summer of 1861. Unwittingly Smith had begun the tourist trade for the Isles of Scilly!

On July 31st July 1872 Augustus Smith died in Plymouth while on his way back to his beloved Scilly. He was buried in the churchyard at St Buryan, a small village in West Cornwall. He had become admired and respected by Scillonians for his work and care over the thirty-eight years of his 'reign'. He had laid the foundations of a magical garden; what he planned and laid out could only have been conceived and executed by someone with his vision, drive and exceptional talent.

Below: Valhalla Figurehead Museum — collection founded by Augustus Smith.

*Right: Thomas
Algernon Dorrien-
Smith on the Top
Terrace in the late
1800s. (Frank
Gibson)*

THOMAS ALGERNON DORRIEN-SMITH

"He devoted his life to these islands."

Augustus Smith died convinced that no member of his family would wish to take on the existing lease and had therefore willed the whole agreement back to the Duchy of Cornwall, provided they agreed to make a payment of £20,000 and £3,000 per year. The rest of his estate was left to his nephew, Thomas Algernon Smith Dorrien Smith, a Lieutenant in the Tenth Hussars. The Duchy refused to take back the lease, so it did indeed fall into the lap of Thomas, who in accordance with his uncle's wishes, now called himself Thomas Algernon Dorrien-Smith.

There was for some time uncertainty as to whether Thomas could afford to take on the burden of the islands but, within two years he had resigned his commission and settled on Tresco as the new Lord Proprietor. In his early days Charles Allen, who had been steward to the islands for twenty years, guided him. Very little changed and the transition from uncle to nephew went very smoothly. At this time Edith Tower came to stay on Tresco as she had done many times before. She wrote many letters to her mother, Lady Sophia Tower, who had been a great confidant and friend of Augustus Smith. Her notes contained details of flowering plants and the growth of her favourite shrubs that grew about the garden. The following year, 1875, Edith and Thomas Algernon were married; this was a happy union: she was as devoted to the islands as she was to him.

Very soon after returning from Paris, having been married only a few weeks previously the couple were to experience a tragedy so typical of Scilly. On May 7th a storm blew a German transatlantic steamer, the *Schiller*, onto the Retarrier ledges close to the Bishop Rock Lighthouse. Thick fog made any sort of rescue impossible, even for Scillonians, until morning light. First news did not reach the Abbey until breakfast time. Two boatloads of half-drowned passengers, 27 in all, arrived in New Grimsby. Thomas Algernon and his brother went directly to the village and took command, and over the next few days made arrangements for both the living and the dead. For many weeks throughout that summer bodies were washed up as a terrible reminder.

It was generally agreed that if there had been a telegraph link to the Bishop Rock, many more lives would have been saved - a point made at the Board of Trade enquiry. As it was, a local company, the Post Office having refused to buy it, funded the link from St Mary's to Penzance and when the cable broke two years later, the islands were completely cut off and the company bankrupted. Only after the most vehement entreaties did the Postmaster General consent and establish a public telegraph. This was the first and by no means the last of the tussles that Dorrien-Smith had with various government departments to obtain proper amenities for the islands. Anyone familiar with the history of the Isles of Scilly will realise that this is an ever-present problem.

Thomas Algernon's arrival coincided with a dramatic downturn in the islands' prosperity - one of the factors in the public telegraph not being introduced. Shipbuilding declined with the advent of steam and iron ships, St Mary's was no longer a port of call, larger vessels calling at Falmouth and beyond instead. In consequence there was no work for the pilots and despite the sea teeming with fish, there was only a local market as there was little means of getting catches to the mainland. In addition the early potato industry was threatened and undercut by the Channel Islands and the Mediterranean: nothing changes!

Happily the solution to the problem was growing wild throughout the islands. There is no record of who first had the idea of sending cut daffodils to the mainland, but certainly Dorrien-Smith was responsible for the development of

Above: Aloe Walk 1873: Mexican Agaves in flower. (Frank Gibson)

THOMAS ALGERNON DORRIEN-SMITH

1. James Jenkins, gardener and head gardener for 62 years until 1927, in Valhalla. (Frank Gibson)

2. Top Terrace and Neptune c1908. (Frank Gibson)

3. Tree Fern Dell adjacent to Valhalla in the late 1800s. (Frank Gibson)

4. Early Garden Photographer c1908. (Robert A. Dorrien-Smith)

5. James Jenkins at the Garden Entrance in the late 1800s waiting to conduct visitors around the Garden. (Frank Gibson)

6. Neptune Steps c1908. (Frank Gibson)

the industry and the turnaround of the islands' economy. A number of farmers and Dorrien-Smith had experimented with sending a few boxes of flowers to Covent Garden, the most famous incident being the consignment sent up by William Trevellick in his wife's hatbox! This was during the last days of Augustus Smith. Trevellick was a shrewd, intelligent, hardworking man who by careful selection built up a store of good quality bulbs. Thomas Algernon saw the potential and decided to act. Scilly had a full month's advantage over everywhere else in the British Isles.

In 1881 he travelled to the Channel Islands, Holland and Belgium to research growing techniques and new varieties, not just for himself but for the good of the Scillonian farming community. Thus the flower industry on Scilly took off. Thomas Algernon devoted thirty acres of ground to narcissus and very quickly farms all over Scilly were following. Only by sheer hard work was it possible to maintain the fields throughout the year. Every two or three years the bulbs needed to be lifted and planted in fresh ground. Glasshouses were erected which were used for bringing forward flowers even earlier than those grown outdoors. Blooms were picked and brought inside, the extra heat from the glass gaining a few precious extra days. At the first flower show held at St Mary's on March 30th 1886 Thomas Algernon exhibited over one hundred and fifty varieties of narcissus. Of all the varieties shown "Soleil d'Or" and "Scilly White" consistently outshone many others both for being early and prolific.

Transport of the flowers in heavy wooden crates was, in the very early days, difficult for the farmers from the off-islands. The Dorrien-Smiths had a steam launch which made things easier but smaller farmers would sometimes miss the steamer sailing to the mainland if bad weather occurred at the last moment and their sailing boats were unable to dock or were simply late. As the industry got bigger it was evi-

dent that the quay on St Mary's was not large enough to take the freight. It was decided to extend the quay and it was agreed that Dorrien-Smith money would fund the work with farmers making a contribution when they made use of the facility. Fishermen also took advantage of the vessels transporting the flower crops to the mainland. Fishing boats from all over the country fished in the south-west waters and used the flower sailings to get catches to the mainland.

The Abbey Garden had by this time been going from strength to strength with many of the plants introduced by Smith reaching maturity and producing flower. The sister of Augustus Smith, Mrs. Frances Le Marchant, captured many of these flowering periods in a series of paintings. Over forty studies were painted between 1873 and 1883 with a remarkable eye for botanical detail. The mixture of plants in each plate shows how diverse the plant collection had already become. A February example shows *Salvia argentea*, Mediterranean dweller, *Hakea denticulata* from the family Proteaceae with pink and white flowers, *Aloe succotrina* one of the multi-stemmed succulent specimens from the South-Western Cape, *Leptospermum scoparium*, one of the Australian tea trees and various *Acacia* species. In October also captured are *Sparmannia africana*, white flowered hemp from South Africa, *Cantua buxifolia,* native of South America, commonly known by the wonderful name - Magic Flower of the Incas. Representing the bulb group is *Schizostylis coccinea* a delicate member of Iridaceae with scarlet red flowers. Protecting these plants were the shelter plantings originated by Augustus Smith.

Thomas Algernon by this time had pinpointed that the two Californian trees, Monterey pine and Monterey cypress

*Left: The East
Rockery today.
(Simon McBride)*

also chosen by Smith, had served their apprenticeships in standing up to the Atlantic gales and so he planted thousands of each on the south west hill. In his time he saw great results from both his and his uncle's work.

In the spring of 1897 the first Spring Flower Show, of which Thomas Algernon was Vice-President, was held at the City Hall, Truro. In the years to come Tresco would make a great contribution from the garden in supporting the annual exhibitions, which in its turn introduced many tender species of plants to Cornish gardens.

Thomas Algernon and his large family of two sons and five daughters lived on Scilly for over forty years. It would have been very easy for him to turn his back on the island community but that was not the Dorrien-Smith way. By following the example set by his uncle, he probably more than anybody secured the islands' future. He died in 1918 and on the family monument that looks from the hillside over the Atlantic Ocean and the Abbey Garden an inscription reads "He devoted his life unselfishly to these islands and added greatly to their prosperity and beauty".

Above: The Pebble Garden c1908. All the stones were gathered from the beaches by the gardeners. (Frank Gibson)

Right: Arthur and Eleanor Dorrien-Smith c1909. (Frank Gibson)

MAJOR A.A. DORRIEN-SMITH

A great plantsman

When his father died in 1918 Major Arthur Dorrien-Smith was already a gardener and horticulturist of some note. While on active service in South Africa between 1899 and 1902 he regularly collected plants or seed of interest from the Veldt, which were sent back to his father for the ever-increasing collection on Tresco. In 1903 while ADC to the Governor General of Australia he was instrumental in helping set up what can be regarded as today's Botanic Garden in Melbourne. In 1907 Captain Arthur, as he was then, joined a scientific expedition to the Auckland and Campbell Islands off New Zealand. The islands were very inhospitable to people but a treasure trove if you were an avid plant collector. *Metrosideros lucida*, a salt resistant tree, was very dominant, with plants of Coprosma, Olearia, Podocarpus and Dacrydium also very prolific. The records are poor and we are unsure as to the survival rate from this trip. However it is recorded that herbarium specimens, which included *Veronica* (Hebe) species from the expedition, are available in Christchurch Museum for those that may wish to see them.

In May of 1909 Arthur Dorrien-Smith married Eleanor Bolby and in late July as an extended honeymoon they took a trip to Western Australia and arrived in Perth having experienced appalling weather en route. After a short stay there they took a ship to Albany from where they began a prolonged camping tour to the Stirling Mountains. Setting off in horse-driven buggies it took two weeks of travel, taking all provisions and water with them, before reaching their destination. Moving through the Australian bush in this manner would have been extremely hot and probably quite uncomfortable. Both Captain Arthur and his wife, who was also a keen plantsperson, were very excited at the variety and range of unfamiliar species. Banksia was prolific and as

they moved between sites they saw large numbers of Hakea, Dryandra, Melaleuca and Leptospermum growing on the roadsides in the sand plains. Anigozanthus the "Kangaroo Paw" was a plant they had not seen before with many *Acacia* species they would not have recognised all growing in profusion. *Eucalyptus* species were in evidence along with lower plants such as Leschenaultia, Sisyrinchium and *Templetonia retusa* a small shrub, known as the "Coral Bush" due to its red flowers. This period was to inspire both Arthur and Eleanor to bring back many new species to the Abbey Garden and to write a paper for the Royal Horticultural Society Journal entitled "A Botanising Expedition to Western Australia in the Spring".

Arthur Dorrien-Smith had an active life in Army service in South Africa, Australia and New Zealand which meant of course he was in the right place to pursue his love of plants and gardens. In 1909 he made a botanic expedition to Chatham Island - this is an island some 48km (30 miles) long, with an area no bigger than 560 square kilometres (350 square miles), 1120km (700 miles) off the coast of New Zealand. It was here that he came across *Olearia semidentata* a plant he was to introduce into Britain upon his return. Planted in 1910, it first flowered on Tresco in 1913.

On one occasion he returned from his plant hunting expeditions with over two thousand living plants growing in pots and many new introductions of seed. As the Panama Canal did not exist the ship came around Cape Horn - not for the faint hearted! Holding cases, constructed for the journey and fixed on deck so that light reached the plants, enabled the specimens to be aired and watered on a daily basis. But sailing conditions sometimes made this impossible and with salt spray and damp conditions many plants did not survive the return journey to Tilbury Docks. Everything brought back was always divided where possible between

Above: December 1929 – The Long Walk after the gales. (Frank Gibson)

Tresco, Edinburgh Botanics and Kew Gardens. As a bonus the boat also brought up to fifty exotic birds for the "Duckery" area in front of Tresco Abbey.

The First World War intervened at this point and took Arthur away from his horticultural interests. His return from the war to Tresco in 1918 sadly coincided with the death of his father. Most of the men on the island had been called to enlist which left very few to do the work and keep the islands running. The war had affected the commercial viability of island farms and in particular the flower and potato industry. Arthur still had the lease for all five inhabited islands and the responsibility that went with it. He devoted considerable financial and personal effort on these problems but found that to run the islands as his father had done was beyond the finance available from the family. In 1922 he gave back responsibility and control of

all but Tresco and the uninhabited islands to the Duchy. However he still had a strong influence as Chairman of the Isles of Scilly Council, a position held for his lifetime.

In the garden Arthur and Eleanor began to make their own impression. The head gardener at the time was Mr James Jenkins who had been working there for well over fifty years. His successor William George Andrews arrived on Tresco in 1922. He was Kew-trained with a particular interest in, and knowledge of, orchids. For a short while the two worked together until the retirement of James Jenkins. At this time any visitors arriving to view the garden would ring a large bell at the entrance of Valhalla which summoned the head gardener who would bid them to sign the Visitors' Book in the Visitors' Room attached to the house. They were then escorted through the garden on a guided tour. Entrance in those days was free but contributions were accepted on behalf of the Tresco Nursing Association, which was headed by Eleanor Dorrien-Smith.

There were sixteen garden staff, each having his own role to play. Besides the normal 'exotic' gardening the household still used the garden to good effect. Melons, peaches and nectarines were grown in the glasshouses. Outdoors apples, pears, plums, strawberries and raspberries flourished. Each morning Mr Andrews took the selection of the season to the Abbey kitchens. A horse and cart was used regularly to collect seaweed from beaches for use as mulch and fertiliser. On Saturday mornings two men swept the full length of the Abbey road, some eight hundred metres, using the old-fashioned besom brooms. This was in preparation for the family to be driven in a horse and carriage to church on Sundays.

At Christmas time Major and Mrs Dorrien-Smith would invite Mr Andrews and other senior members of staff with their families to the Abbey. The children danced around the candle-lit Christmas tree and all would be given a gift. In many ways things have not changed all that much. In the present day on Christmas Eve the island carol singers are invited to the Abbey to sing before delicately wolfing down platefuls of hot mince pies, sausage rolls and sherry.

Another interesting comparison between then and now can be seen in the twinning of Tresco Abbey Garden and the garden at La Mortola on the Italian Riviera belonging to the Hanbury family. In 1920 Sir Arthur Hill, Director of the Royal Botanic Gardens, Kew published an article in the *Kew Bulletin* coupling the gardens together. The same paper concluded by describing Tresco Abbey Garden as "An imperial asset of great importance to the botanists of this country whose work lies with the botanical resources of the British Empire". Both had magnificent plant collections and

*Left: 1927 –
James Jenkins the
'old' head
gardener and
Andrews, the new.
(G.J.King)*

Major A.A. Dorrien-Smith

1: Snow February 1934. Robert is just home from India. (Robert A. Dorrien-Smith)

2: December 1929. Clearing up after the gales. (Frank Gibson)

3: December 1929. The Long Walk after the gales. (Frank Gibson)

4: The Pebble Garden, 1920. (Frank Gibson)

5: Abbey Garden: the Long Walk looking west in the1920s. (Frank Gibson)

32

both grew plants of a similar nature but with very different climatic conditions.

In December 1929 the garden was hit by storm force winds. After five days with wind speeds up to 110 miles an hour, large areas of the windbreaks and most of the garden were devastated. Over six hundred mature trees were lost as the wind changed direction three times. The wind speed did not drop below an estimated seventy miles an hour. Both Major and Mrs Dorrien-Smith were away but kept informed of the tree losses by telegram. Many of the plants were crushed or smashed beyond repair, but the estate workers and garden staff quickly cleared the paths to create some sort of order. In fact it was very soon recognised as a bonus in many ways, for as trees were lost in the lower section of the garden, the higher light levels meant that many new plantings flourished which otherwise would have sat in deep shade.

Where trees had fallen on the Abbey hillsides the Major left many of the fallen branches and canopies to protect the new plantings. His eldest daughter, Anne, born in 1911, tells us that wire was strung from tree to tree and branches suspended to form fence-like shelters and new young trees were planted inside the protection of these fallen giants. All of his seven children, Robert, Anne, Tom, Innes, Lionel, Frances and Helen were enlisted to help restore the gar-

Below right: 1931- Estate workers at the coming of age of the Major's eldest son Robert who was killed in the Second World War. Front Row — Major with stick — to right Commander Tom Dorrien-Smith, James Jenkins; to left Robert. (Frank Gibson)

Below: 1934, the Middle Terrace. (Robert A. Dorrien-Smith)

32

den's shelter. The youngest daughter, Helen recalls helping her father in the glasshouses on many occasions potting up plants. Her only problem she remembers, is that she could hardly see over the bench at the tender age of six!

Over the next few years the Major introduced many new plants to the garden and in 1935 a list of plants cultivated on Tresco was compiled. The estimate was very close to three thousand five hundred species and varieties. Major Arthur regularly ordered plants from the well-known New Zealand nursery of Duncan and Davies which specialised in native trees and shrubs, acquiring many rare and unusual plants for Tresco. Letters tell us of *Freycinetia banksii*, a dracaena-like plant, being ordered for the collection with a

Below: Andrews on the Middle Terrace. (G.J.King)

Grecian Rock Terrace Tresco.
photo. C.J.King & Son Scilly. G.43.

Above: Major Arthur and **Mexican Furcreas** *in June 1944. (Robert A. Dorrien-Smith)*

Right: Major Arthur Dorrien-Smith uncharacteristically hatless. (Robert A. Dorrien-Smith)

reply on growing hints from Mr Davies himself. *Cyathea medullaris* and *Meryta sinclairii* were sent in the same order, all to be grown in the damp and shady parts of the garden. Some of the more outstanding groups of plants growing at this time included sixty nine species of Mexican *Agave*, one hundred and fifty nine species and varieties of *Pelargonium*, thirty nine species of *Acacia* from Australia, twenty eight species of Australian *Hakea*, fourteen species of *Banksia*; Echium from the Canary Islands numbered seven species, one of which was the red biannual, *Echium wildpretii*; four species of the wonderful *Metrosideros* trees from New Zealand; a staggering one hundred and fifty three species of *Mesembryanthemum*, the succulent group from South Africa, and sixty species of *Aloe*, succulents from the same region.

In just six short years the garden had been restored some way towards its former glory.

The outbreak of the Second World War again meant that call-up to the services took many islanders away from Tresco. The garden staff went down from sixteen to five; the Major did most of the plant propagation himself and often returned with his wife into the garden after dinner to attend the plants. Mrs Dorrien-Smith through the war years also took on her responsibilities, running the island hospital, the Red Cross and taking charge of the Land Girls. Any garden visitors were asked to make a contribution towards the Dorrien-Smith Nursing Association, which provided both Bryher and Tresco with a nursing service. One very dry August day during the war a small number of incendiaries were dropped setting fire to a specimen of *Pinus radiata* but Mrs Dorrien-Smith was on hand to put the fire out with the help of her stirrup pump. A fire could have spread through the hill with dire consequences.

World War II was to have a lasting and sad impact on the family. Three of the Major's four sons, Robert, Lionel and Francis were killed while fighting for their country. The family memorial in Tresco Church records that two brothers, Robert and Lionel tragically died on the same day in France. Robert the eldest son was never able to take over his father's mantle; he had already begun to develop a keen interest in horticulture. In 1934 at the age of twenty-four, while with the Army in India, family letters tell us he had collected bulbs of *Tulipa lanata* from a vineyard north of Kabul which he sent back to his father who in turn passed them on to Kew Gardens for identification and recording. It is a great pity he was not able to fulfil his horticultural destiny.

After the war the Major planted many unusual plants within the shelterbelts: *Acacias* of many species including, *Acacia floribunda*, *Acacia cultriformis* and *Acacia decurrens*.

Members of the Proteaceae were tried with great success; *Protea neriifolia*, has always thrived on Tresco's soil. It was also recognised that many self-sown seedlings were beginning to appear in great numbers on the hillsides: notably *Metrosideros excelsa*, the New Zealand Christmas Tree, well known for its tolerance to salt spray, *Clethra arborea* from Madeira and *Acacia longifolia* from Australia.

In the early 1950s Major Arthur opened the garden to the paying public by introducing an entrance charge of 2/6. In the past it had been free or through the contribution box. His daughter, Helen Dorrien-Smith, tells us that at the time he was so concerned about this obligatory fee that he spent the whole summer accosting visitors and inquiring if they felt it was value for money - I am sure it was!

On one of their final collecting trips abroad the Major and Mrs Dorrien-Smith took a trip on the ship *Winchester Castle* to South Africa and were away for three months. They returned with many new seeds from the Cape flora to enhance the garden. The Major quite rightly was acknowledged by the Royal Horticultural Society by being awarded the V.M.H. - the Victoria Medal of Honour which was established in 1897 and enables the Council of the R.H.S to confer conspicuous honour on British horticulturists. At any one time there are only sixty-three holders representing each year of Queen Victoria's reign. Major Arthur Dorrien-Smith was a worthy recipient.

Above: The Middle Terrace today.

T. M. DORRIEN-SMITH

Consolidation and commerce

In 1955 Lieutenant Commander Thomas Mervyn Dorrien-Smith succeeded his father. He did not come to Tresco as a plantsman but in a very short time came to love every minute spent learning and caring about his new charge. He had a very good eye for choosing the right plant for the right place so that it made a statement in the garden. Quite quickly he looked at the island's commercial infrastructure and made a conscious decision to make the transition from a purely agricultural community to one that also embraced tourism. This did not mean abandoning farming but finding a balance between both industries. Garden visitor numbers were up to seventeen thousand per annum but this was still not enough for the garden to sustain itself without extra financial input from the family coffers. If the garden was to continue as a focal point for the tourist industry then a realistic entrance charge would have to be made. In 1958 a small number of island cottages were let during the summer; all were quite basic and not up to the standard of today's time-share properties, but comfortable enough for the family summer holiday. This was supplemented by the building of the Island Hotel in Old Grimsby, which was completed in 1960, using the old coastguard cottages as the basis to build upon. All of these measures served to add to the income of the island. This ensured the very existence of the garden. At one point it was possible that the garden would become part of the Royal Botanic Garden group attached to Kew. Happily the garden stayed under family control.

Tom Dorrien Smith always maintained very strong ties between Abbey family life and the garden. This was seen as both normal and very important. He had five children, who were all born on Tresco between 1946 and 1956: Teona, Alexandra, Robert, Charlotte and James. They were all encouraged to participate in the practical side of the garden.

The necessary thinning of the vast areas inhabited by the *Rhododendron ponticum* made the Abbey hillside a popular place to work. Each of the children had his or her own axe and billhook. The 'Guv', as his children called him, was always pleased when his family helped. The Top Terrace was a favourite area with many of his South African Protea, Erica and Leucadendron being planted by the children.

His daughter Teona, the eldest child, told me that traditionally on Sunday mornings the children would pick flowers from the garden to make buttonholes for the family and friends to wear to church. The drawing room window was always kept full of fifteen to twenty specimen vases of typical and rare examples of flowers from the garden for discussion and admiration. There were no cars on Tresco and normal transport for the family was pony and cart driven by the groom dressed in bowler hat and breeches. The groom at the time was an ex-Indian army Sergeant Major called John Dibble. A black and white open carriage was used for Royal visits and special occasions. In 1965 it was again used for the Archbishop of Canterbury who came to hold a special service in the Old Abbey under umbrellas in the pouring rain.

Commander Tom, as he became known, was a great lover of the islands and in his time became the elected Chairman of the Isles of Scilly Council - unlike his ancestors who were hereditary chairmen. He hoped that he was doing the right thing for Scilly and wondered if his decisions were the same as those his late brother Robert might have made.

Over a period of years The Commander played host to many royal and ministerial visits. Her Majesty The Queen, Prince Philip, Prince Charles and Princess Anne were guests in 1967. The Queen Mother also made the first of two visits, the second being in 1985 arriving in the Royal Yacht *Britannia*. Mrs Thatcher made an official visit to the Isles of Scilly while she was Minister for Education.

Above: Flower picking in the late 1950s: everyone was required to help including boatmen, gardeners and estate workers. (Lawry)

Commander Tom was the first member of the family to bring the British Airways helicopter into Tresco. He arranged for up to fifty of Cornwall's garden owners to make a special day visit to Tresco: many of them for the first time. The month of July was chosen so his guests were able to view the legendary New Zealand pohutukawa trees in full flower. We hear, as an added bonus, *Eucalyptus ficifolia* also happened to be in fine form at the same time, its scarlet red flowers peeping over the wall from the shelterbelts. One of those invited guests, Nigel Holman, remembers that it was a glorious summer's day with two trips needed by the helicopter to transport Cornwall's finest. Both flights landed on the site of the present heliport on the fringe of the garden. Commander Tom and his wife Tamara guided the group through the garden in the morning followed by a magnificent lunch on the terrace of the Abbey. Among the guests were Major General E.G.W.W. Harrison of Tremeer, Major Walter Magor of Lamellen, Nigel and Elizabeth Holman of Chyverton, Simon and Elizabeth Bolitho of Trengwainton and Mrs Alison Johnstone, wife of George Johnstone of Trewithen. From the Scottish Island of Gigha, Lord Horlick had also made the journey. An added house guest at the time was Lord Talbot de Malahide from Malahide Castle, Dublin, who, on the group's arrival, was standing next to the Commander in an upright manner and was promptly mistaken for the house butler and handed all the coats. I hope they tipped him! We are reliably informed in the afternoon that among the ladies in the group a small detachment tucked skirts into knickers for some dignified paddling on one of the sandy Tresco beaches.

At this period the windbreaks were nearing the peak of their maturity; if the Commander had a blind spot it was in failing to see the necessity for replanting and replacement of the shelter. Many areas were being shaded-out by the tree canopy which prevented young trees or even seedlings from growing efficiently. A high percentage of the trees were the same age and in later years this was to cause a problem when the storms hit, the result being that everything fell over at the same time.

In 1963 the Commander and his mother Eleanor took a trip virtually retracing the 1909 footsteps of Major A.A. Dorrien-Smith; they made the journey to Western Australia, Perth and King's Park Garden before visiting all the major botanic gardens on the eastern Australian coast. We have extensive notes of the plants collected in the Stirling Mountains, Lake Grace, Albany and Cape Naturalste. Chamaelaucium, Andersonia, Patersonia, Dryandra, Hibbertia, Calytrix, Goodenia, Pimelea, Baeckea, Beaufortia, Darwinia, Leucopogon, Grevillea and Oxylobium were amongst the two hundred and twenty specimens gathered. Duplicate plants were presented to King's Park Botanic Garden with the main collection being destined for Tresco. The two of them then travelled on to visit other major botanic gardens in Adelaide, Melbourne, Canberra, Sydney and Brisbane. *Banksia* species were a particular favourite of the Commander and he introduced many new species to the garden. One that always stands out when in flower is *Banksia coccinea,* its bright red terminal flowers perched on the branch like gas burners. Similar visits were made in New Zealand to Auckland, Dunedin, Timaru, Wellington and Christchurch Botanics. The Dorrien-Smiths also took the opportunity to call at the well-known nursery of Duncan and Davies to view and purchase plants to be sent back to Tresco. One notable plant on the invoice list was *Xeronema callistemon*, the Poor Knight's Lily, a perennial in the family Liliaceae which actually flowered on Tresco, for the first time, we think, in the summer of 1999 with its long red stemmed flowers emerging from the strap-like leaves.

The Commander and his second wife Peggy visited South Africa in 1969 and brought back plants from the Cape that

TRESCO ABBEY PRIVATE GARDENS

These Gardens are maintained by Lt. Comdr. Dorrien Smith for National, Local and Botanical interests.

OPEN WEEKDAYS ONLY
10 a.m. to 4 p.m.

Admission 5/-   Children 1/-
Weekly Tickets 7/6

For DAY EXCURSION VISITOR from Penzance the Steamship Company's Tresco Excursion Ticket admits.

Permanent Island Residents admitted Free during Official Opening Times, also Sundays.

All are welcome but must take care not to pick flowers either inside or outside the gates, as many are planted for naturalisation.

People are not allowed to sit around and eat food in the Gardens, nor are they allowed to sketch without permission.

FIRES — Cigarette ends are very dangerous; the vegetation on all the Islands is very inflammable. Do not attempt to light any fires anywhere.

T. M. DORRIEN SMITH, Lt. Comdr.

A. H. READ & SON, PRINTERS, ST. MARY'S.

Above centre: Early publicity, 1960s.

Below centre: The Commander and the Queen Mother on School Green, Tresco for the May Day dancing. 1960s. (Lawry)

have so much become part of the Tresco story: Protea, Leucadendrom, Leucospermum, Cape Erica, Gladiolus, Aristea, Podalyria, Aloe, Arctotis, Virgilia, Galtonia and Watsonia are just a small selection from his collecting exploits. He is also credited with the introduction of *Osteospermum* "Tresco Peggy", named after his wife. It is an enthusiastic and sun loving plant that will produce a vivid purple flower that sits above its foliage, right through the year. (It is also freely available as "Tresco Purple" or "Nairobi Purple" in the nursery trade.) In the early 1960s he exhibited the full range of the garden treasures at the Chelsea Flower Show. Every specimen was as a cut flower and so had to last not only the journey but five days in a vase in the heat of the vast show marquee. *Puya chilensis* from the mountains of Chile, *Protea* and *Aloe* species from the Cape, South Africa, *Acacia* and *Banksia* from Australia, *Cyathea* and *Dicksonia* from New Zealand and *Agave* and *Yucca* from North America and Mexico were all successfully taken to the show.

Head gardener at the time was John Smith. He and gardeners Frank Naylor and David Hopkins cut and packed all material and journeyed by Scillonian from St Mary's to Penzance and onto London by train, arriving at nearly midnight. They were met at the station by the Commander and driven across London only to find the site locked. Various gates were rattled and security men roused until entry was gained so eventually the Tresco contingent made their grand entrance at one o'clock in the morning. Having delivered the exhibit to the main show tent Commander Tom went to his club for the night while the gardeners settled for blankets from the First Aid Tent and slept, by their own choice, under the exhibit! Surprisingly for May it was extremely cold and head gardener John Smith, we are informed, kept his feet warm that night by putting them in a barrel of dry beech leaves!

One of the Commander's most enjoyable moments was to give a lecture to the Royal Horticultural Society at Vincent Square, London, on April 30th 1968. He told the full Tresco story, starting not unsurprisingly with the contribution of Augustus Smith, running through the generations and finishing with an imaginary garden walk taking his audience on a tour of his plant collection. Older members still recall the passion and enthusiasm of that talk and the enduring memory of his love for his garden. He had a great attachment to Tresco and would be always evident at island functions taking a leading role in the proceedings. From garden fetes to school treats his influence and enjoyment were a dominant feature.

*Left: First flowering of the **Xeronema callistemon** in the Garden in 1999. Plants were introduced by the Commander from the Duncan and Davies Nursery, New Zealand.*

*Right: Prince
Charles and Robert
Dorrien-Smith
1982 on the
Middle Terrace.
(Frank Gibson)*

ROBERT A. DORRIEN-SMITH

Innovation and security

When Augustus Smith began his garden on the site of the St Nicholas' Priory he could not possibly have imagined that it would grow into what we see today. Five direct generations down the line Robert Dorrien-Smith and his family still enjoy and care for the garden, but with the far wider range of activities and responsibilities that are integral to the management of a modern day amenity garden and botanic establishment.

Tresco Abbey Garden holds a unique position in the horticultural world, yet still manages to be a genuine family garden as well as being a business that helps to maintain not just the garden, but which assists the whole island community including families who have lived on the island for many generations.

Over the years each leading family member has made a significant contribution to the garden and, carrying on that tradition, Robert Dorrien-Smith has by careful management introduced a structure that will sustain both the garden and island for the foreseeable future.

When taking over the running of the island from his father in the early 1970s Robert was able to rely on then head gardener Peter Clough to steer the garden in the right direction. This gave him time to find his feet. In this period the windbreaks were probably at their peak and the plant collections inside the garden perimeter under Peter's management were in prime health and well-documented. Thus Robert was able to make himself familiar with the workings of the island and ease his way into the mysteries of his horticultural inheritance knowing it was in safe hands.

Robert Dorrien-Smith has overcome the 1987 snow damage and the 1990 hurricane, both unprecedented disasters that so devastated the garden. The plant collection has now, at the beginning of the new century, been successfully replaced and the windbreaks are flourishing with the replanting of sixty thousand young trees. From day one after the storms, Robert with daily meetings personally oversaw the planning and planting of the new shelterbelts: he went out and about with forester Steve Parkes to ensure that there was continuity for the future

A major influence on the garden and island in recent years has been the introduction of the helicopter service from Penzance. We believe this is the only garden in the world to have its own direct helicopter link. The heliport was introduced to Tresco in 1983 and opened by the chairman of British Airways, Lord King. The Tresco Estate maintains and trains its own staff under the strict rules of the Civil Aviation Authority. It has often caused some amusement to passengers checking in for flights to learn the control tower on Tresco was in an earlier life the garden tea hut. Not to be outdone the landing square also doubles up as the island cricket pitch. On the odd occasion stumps have been drawn to allow flights to land and passengers clapped in before bowling can be resumed!

It is also not unknown for the complete ground crew of Air Traffic Control and three fire crew to be made up by our own garden staff. Living on a small island dictates that islanders are proficient in many different skills. Each year rigorous training in fire and first-aid takes place. On early mornings throughout the year head gardener Andrew Lawson and propagator Dave Inch can often be seen in full fire uniform dragging heavy hose pipes through the sand dunes in mock-up training sessions. These periods are often a lot of fun and go to break up the daily routine.

Each 'department' works hand in hand to form one large unit working together. The introduction of holidays for garden lovers at both the Island Hotel and The New Inn have proved popular. Residential garden lectures take place regularly and guided tours by one of the Tresco gardeners are

Above: The Abbey 1999.
(G.K.N.Westland)

always popular with our visitors. By its own choice Tresco will never be overrun with visitors, but the modest and controlled numbers that do visit maintain the required balance that is so important. Even the modern garden shop and entrance introduced in 1983 by Robert has already been overwhelmed and plans are in place to develop a new visitor centre.

Throughout the short history of the garden each member of the Dorrien-Smith family has always introduced a personal touch. It is not easy to leave a mark on a well-established and laid-out garden. Designs set in place over previous years do not always leave much room for manoeuvre in the present day. Robert and Lucy Dorrien-Smith have however made a big impression with our visitors by their exciting addition to the garden of sculptures and by the major re-landscaping, designing and planting of the new "Mediterranean Garden".

The first important piece of sculpture was positioned in an area that had always been affectionately known to the gardeners as 'The Jam Tart': a circular bed of fuchsias erring somewhat on the colourful side. The sculpture by David Wynne was formed from a block of multi-coloured South African marble which was a present to the sculptor from George Harrison of the Beatles. David's wife Gilli posed for the piece which was named 'Gaia' after the goddess of the earth.

Top right: Mike Nelhams and **Monterey Cypress** *and* **Pines** *in 1992, showing their growth in eight years. (Frank Gibson)*

Right: Building the pergola, 1985. (Roy Cooper)

43

Left: 'Gaia' by David Wynne.

Weighing in at some one-and-a-half tons it meant the skills and time of many people were needed to site it in its final resting place. Paths were widened, plinths constructed (more than once!) and heavy lifting gear put in place prior to her appearance. There are no cranes on Tresco and because of the inaccessible position, a tripod was made from three large cupressus trees up to 9m (30ft) tall which were cut from the Abbey woodland - necessary in any case as part of woodland management! - and block and tackle attached. The tripod was then secured to nearby palm trees for extra stability. When the statue arrived on the scene she was hauled up a sloping path towards the site on an ancient garden trolley by four willing gardeners: they looked and felt much like Egyptian slaves on extra pyramid building duty! In charge of operations was island engineer Dennis Jenkins who had every confidence in his heavy lifting skills. Chewing on his pipe he gave the impression of a man on a Sunday stroll, not a person about to launch an expensive sculpture on a short but perilous journey. For a brief moment when swinging in mid-air to the plinth breaths were held. However ropes stayed intact and tripods stood firm as 'Gaia' safely nestled into place. The stone has a very tactile quality and easy access makes it possible to touch and feel 'Gaia's' contours. It has always been felt that after the terrible damage inflicted by the snow she was, by her timing and introduction, a symbol for the re-awakening of the garden. In her final position in the centre of the garden we feel she has found her perfect setting.

Following hot on the heels of 'Gaia', David Wynne was again commissioned by Robert to produce a life size bronze of his three children Adam, Francis and Michael entitled 'Tresco Children'. The piece was to be placed at the lower end of the most important vista in the garden replacing a historic but rather dull lighthouse cresset believed to be one of the first in the British Isles. The beacon was removed and dispatched to a more suitable site in the Valhalla Figurehead Museum - where for a time it served very nicely as a giant litter bin filled with the remnants of lunch baskets by inconsiderate picnic groups!

What is now known as the "Mediterranean Garden" came about when this large area of the garden was devastated to a degree that entailed complete refurbishment. Robert and Lucy made the decision to make a radical contribution rather than simply replace with similar trees, shrubs and lower vegetation to those lost in the storms. At the western end of the long walk a substantial area was levelled and cleared ready for construction. A bare canvas was laid before us for consideration and planning.

In any established garden it is never easy after one hun-

dred and seventy years to make a radical change that will still fit in with the resident garden features. A design was engineered that gave a series of terraces and new artistic features. All the stone used on the project was island or Cornish granite and has blended into the rest of the garden extremely well.

Building took place over two years with hard landscaping coming first and all design lines centred on an exciting life-size bronze replica of an agave plant, which carried on the general theme of sculptures around the garden. Local artist and sculptor Tom Leaper designed and installed the agave, which also serves as an effective water fountain. Water from this is pumped back up the hill to a sculpted female head and hands which Maria Heitel, mother of Lucy Dorrien-Smith, presented to the garden.

Above and below: The making of the Mediterranean Garden May/June 1992/3

Left: Fountain by Tom Leaper.

Left: The finished Mediterranean Garden. (Derek Harris)

48

Plants to fill the garden were to come from many sources far and wide. A group of olive trees were introduced into the design so that over a period of many years they may give shade and a feel of Mediterranean slopes and hillsides. The olives came from an Italian nursery called Torsanlorenzo on the outskirts of Rome, which provides Mediterranean container-grown trees. Rosemary, lavender and South African scented Pelargoniums were added to provide scent and "Judas" trees planted to give early spring colour with magenta-pink flowers. For the summer months large drifts of Mesembryanthemum and Crassula mixed with *Argyranthemum frutescens* provide banks of colour. In the lower shadier areas, all fighting for position, sit Californian ceanothus, Mediterranean cork oaks and The St Helena ebony with its pink trumpet-like flowers. Later in the year and during the winter months South African Aloes send up red flower spikes above succulent, glossy, green leaves. The garden may be entered from five different paths, each giving a new perspective. Above the bronze agave at the top of the garden is a small open-fronted gazebo which has been decorated in shells and mosaic tiles by Lucy Dorrien-

Top right: Lucy Dorrien-Smith working on the Shell House.

Right: The vegetable, fruit and flower garden. (Derek Harris)

Smith; around its walls individual tiles are dedicated to members of the family. In front of this lies a large open area that has been created for outdoor performances. The overall effect has been very pleasing and will continue to develop over the years. Plans are already in place to continue the vista and paths in a southerly direction towards a new "Bamboo Garden" and to the existing vegetable, fruit and flower garden.

As a private and family garden Tresco has always maintained a large area of produce. In the period of Major A.A. Dorrien-Smith and Commander Tom Dorrien-Smith areas within the garden were used for fruit, flower and vegetables. Fruit cages sat alongside shrub borders and cut flowers grew surrounded by exotics. In the early seventies Robert Dorrien-Smith moved all vegetable, fruit and cut flower cultivation to the west end of the garden where vegetables had been grown in the early years. All of the fruit and vegetables are organically grown with compost from the main gardens. As well as this are the hives and bees that produce Tresco honey, unique in flavour due to the choice of flowers available to our bees. Protea, Eucalyptus and Puya are some of the plants that may be visited by our buzzing hymenopterous friends. Robert, Lucy and the children, Marina and Tristan, visit this area daily.

The long-term success of the garden can be seen in the continuity that still runs through not just the Dorrien-Smith family but also in the garden staff. In very recent years Frank Naylor, David Hopkins, Clarence Handy and Dick Bird, all now retired, had well over 120 years of service between them. Frank Naylor was awarded the R.H.S. long service medal for his lifetime's work in the Abbey Garden.

Gardening has become very much an international and fashionable profession. Now seed and plant exchange have entered the computer age with e-mail being used to publicise seed and plant availability which previously might have taken months. Exchange of information between gardens moves freely and quickly. Many of the Abbey gardeners travel around the world lecturing or leading garden tours. This has huge benefits for the garden. The publicity and stimuli of making contacts when visiting new gardens is invaluable in widening our knowledge and experience.

The media has always been fascinated by the Tresco phenomenon and we are very grateful for it. Publicity ensures that visitor numbers and interest are maintained and steadily increased. Equally important is to be true to the spirit of the garden and not to devalue the work of those who laboured through the years. It is a balance that Robert Dorrien-Smith has achieved to secure the long-term future of the garden and island.

Above: Tresco honey has a flavour all of its own, due to the unique mix of sub-tropical plants.

Left: The Queen Mother (June 1985) Mike Nelhams and Robert Dorrien-Smith admiring **Greyia sutherlandii** *from Natal. (Frank Gibson)*

THE GARDEN

STUDENT DAYS

I was lucky enough to begin my early training in horticulture at the Royal Horticultural Gardens, Wisley, Surrey. In 1976 I was awarded a twelve-month scholarship by the Studley College Trust to work with the garden team headed by the then head gardener, Peter Clough. I had spent a number of summers on the Isles of Scilly, I was fairly familiar with the geography of Tresco, but still had a great sense of excitement at the thought of having a chance to study at this world-renowned horticultural extravaganza.

After a three hour trip on the *M V Scillonian* from Penzance and a short ten-minute launch ride from the main island of St Mary's, I was met by Peter on a wet, foggy, September Saturday afternoon at the quayside on Tresco. Our mode of transport was to be the faithful and rather aged Massey Ferguson tractor and transport box. Myself, suitcase, rucksack and box of garden books were hurled into the back of the box, lifted into the air and bounced across the island in fine style. We came to a halt outside of what was to become my home for the next twelve months, a long, single-storey building named 'The Bothy'. My first impression was of a fearful noise made by some unseen engine. I asked Peter about the fearful racket and he said it was the main generator that supplied the electricity for the island. Having established what it was, I asked Peter if the engine went all day. Peter's reply, with a big grin on his face, was 'Yes and all night. It runs twenty-four hours a day. Enjoy your night's sleep. Welcome to Tresco!' I did not know it at the time but the next two and a half years were to have an overriding influence on my life.

Over the last twenty-five years Studley College Trust students have become a regular feature in the life of the garden. They are chosen at the Royal Horticultural Society headquarters in London by interview each year in April; competition is fierce. Prospective students are from many backgrounds and have many levels of experience.

Applications flood in from Kew, R.H.S. Wisley, Edinburgh Botanics and most of the regional horticultural colleges across the country. Studley has a policy that rules out no one and the choice of student is decided on the day with many factors being involved in the decision. In recent years, due to the generosity of Studley, Tresco has been given the chance to take two students each year to the benefit of both students and garden.

From the very beginning of their time in the garden each student is expected to be fully involved in the practical side of the gardening tasks that lie ahead. Working under the guidance of the head gardener and his team, Tresco offers a student a unique opportunity. He or she is able to experience the care and maintenance of an outstanding collection growing out-of-doors: this never seems to fail to ignite a raw enthusiasm among each yearly intake.

Coming from the 'mainland' to live on a small island only two miles long can still be sometimes a daunting prospect and it is up to us to ensure that our new arrivals are made to feel welcome. The students begin in September when the garden still has much to offer with visitors still plentiful. With shorter days, dark evenings and possible wet weather the island can take on a less friendly atmosphere. Cycling to the local shop at the end of the day, in pitch darkness, on a rusting bike with no light or brakes, for a loaf of bread and a newspaper (both possibly two days old, if the helicopter has not flown) does make one think if the right career decision has been made and perhaps the offer of the job in computers and a warm, cosy office should have been taken after all!

The winter months give the Abbey gardeners a chance to attack the projects that in the spring and summer would

Above:
The Pebble
Garden.

not be possible because of visitors. Areas may be redeveloped or landscaped with the complete garden team taking part. This is a good time to assess the skills of the incoming students. It is stressed to the student that the emphasis is on practical work and an all-round competence level is expected. Tractors and trailers, lawnmowers, sprayers, brushcutters, leafblowers, shredders and hedgetrimmers are all used. Within the glasshouse department seed sowing, cuttings and plant production, both for garden planting and sales, are undertaken.

All plants grown in the glasshouses are for garden planting. We do not use the protection of the glasshouses to hold tender plants that will not grow outside all year round. We test our growing limits with plants on the fringe of our climatic zone; this of course leads to some failures, but that is the exciting challenge in a garden such as Tresco. This ensures that students see the progress from seed to mature plant in the garden.

Students may wonder what they have let themselves in for when they are asked to dig out by hand a large and stubborn tree stump in a force seven gale and lashing rain, or perhaps find themselves at the top of a 9m (30ft) high oak hedge with a rather heavy hedge trimmer. Through the winter months every terrace, walk and shrub border is worked upon. By cleaning, pruning, mulching and planting the student becomes familiar with our style of gardening.

One of the most important skills to be learnt is in rela-

Right: Trimming the evergreen oak (Quercus ilex): the students' annual challenge. Far Right: Only on Tresco would these be weeds. Agapanthus and Aeonium.

tion to the natural seedling production. A high percentage of the garden flora will scatter itself across the garden. *Geranium maderense*, from Madeira, *Agapanthus orientalis* and *Senecio glastifolius* from South Africa are good examples of this. Each of these needs to be thinned, removed completely or left alone to develop. The staff and students need to make decisions in each area while working through the winter overhaul. The result will determine the look for the following season and is therefore highly important.

The study of formal theory is not expected as part of our year, but on many occasions our students are in the middle of a three or four-year diploma or degree so will have been laden with assignments as course work. Management plans, plant identification and conservation work and many other projects can be worked into their gardening year.

Exchange visits with other gardens and horticultural institutions have become an integral part of the student year. For up to three weeks a year our students will take time to gain practical experience elsewhere. In the past Wisley, Rosemoor, Trebah and the Royal Botanic Gardens, Kew have been involved in exchanges. No practical experience is ever wasted and different methods and new techniques can always be called upon at a later date.

Far left: **Senecio glastiifolius**: *a calendar shot for Singapore Airlines, but still weeds to us!*

Left: Echium & Geranium: more weeds!

Right: Phoenix palm in the foreground and **Jubea chilensis** *the Chilean wine palm.*

Seed collection is an important task that often befalls the student. Over the course of the year the plants need to be watched and seed harvested at the right time. We produce a biannual seed exchange list that is compiled and designed by the Studley trainees. As applications from the botanic gardens come in, responsibility for packing, recording and dispatching is given to the students. This process is a great help to them in learning about gardens of the world and their climatic zones.

My own particular year was a memorable one under the supervision of Peter Clough, head gardener on Tresco from 1973 to 1984, who had come from the garden of Sir James Horlick on the Island of Gigha on the West Coast of Scotland. As a plantsman gardener he had the ability to transmit his enthusiasm and personal views in a way that always had students wanting more.

The range of plants growing in the garden is often totally unfamiliar to new students. Most having been brought up on a staple diet of hardy plants and it can be quite a shock to encounter succulents from South Africa, the Canary Islands and Mexico.

All the gardeners are encouraged to answer visitors' enquiries and therefore accurate plant identification is of paramount importance. Working with experienced gardeners, it is a skill usually quickly acquired, although it is not unknown for new students to be standing beaming and

Above: Inside the Old Abbey. (Derek Harris)

*Left: Head gardener Andrew Lawson cleaning the head of **Phoenix canariensis**.*

proud next to a well pruned plant, (or hacked into oblivion) only to find on the arrival of the head gardener that the specimen 'next door' was the actual patient to be treated. Exit student, head bowed!

At least once a year the Abbey Garden attends either a national or regional flower show. Though we plan the content, size, design and shape in advance, the weather immediately beforehand decides what materials are actually used.

On most occasions it will be the head gardener and student who will cut, pack, transport, build and man the exhibit. Cutting the plants will start early in the morning and by lunchtime the tool shed will often contain lorryloads of foliage and flowers making it resemble a tropical rainforest. All material has to be cut as freshly as possible to be able to survive the packing, travel, unpacking and arranging. Usually the exhibits will need to last up to three days of public scrutiny before inevitably wilting.

In 1985 I decided that a trip to the Royal Horticultural Spring Show in London could be attempted. It meant that we would have to have a top class exhibit, but we felt we were up to the task. I had impressed upon our staff the need for good clean material with 'that something extra' if we could find it. John Lanyon, the student of the year, had joined us from Wisley Gardens and was always keen to impress. Imagine my horror when walking beneath a 27m (90ft) tall specimen of Norfolk Island Pine, I was called from the top of its branches. He had taken me at my word: there swaying in the breeze on the flimsiest of boughs was John, grinning and brandishing a cluster of cones for the exhibit! He did not have a parachute, so had to content himself with climbing back down to earth. This sort of attitude must have paid off because we were awarded an RHS Gold Medal and a further award for the best exhibit of its type for the year.

My own show experience as a Studley/Tresco student took me in 1977 to the Cornwall Garden Society Show, then held in the Truro City Hall. Having done all the hard work of cutting and packing, we set sail on the boat to Penzance from where we were collected and driven to Truro. Peter Clough and myself were very kindly 'put up' by the ex-Director of Rosewarne Horticultural Research Station, Camborne, Fred Shepherd. Breakfasts with Fred always took on a horticultural slant with discussions ranging from windbreaks and salt spray tolerance to the burning agricultural question - 'Would you kindly pass the boiled eggs please?'

The venue was bursting with exhibits from across the County and being Jubilee Year there seemed to be an awful lot of red, white and blue. Many of the well known Cor-

nish gardeners were moving about the hall, Nigel Holman from Chyverton with his magnolias, Peter Horder, head gardener from Trengwainton with his mixed shrubs and Major Walter Magor striding through the rows of rhododendron exhibits checking that nothing exceeded the regulation size for its class. Peter Borlase, then head gardener at Lanhydrock House, could always be relied upon to take home armfuls of cups for the National Trust.

It was traditional on the Sunday afternoon of the show weekend to visit gardens. I was invited to Tregothnan, home of Lord and Lady Falmouth. Also in the group was Mr. H. E. Boscawen, brother to Lord Falmouth, for whom, at a later stage in my career, I was to work for five years in his Sussex garden High Beeches.

As a student, if you are lucky, the best way to visit a garden is with the owner or head gardener. The more interesting plants are pointed out, cutting material is sometimes offered and a new contact is made for plant exchange in the future. On this visit a vast thick stemmed tree *Quercus suber*, the cork oak, is the specimen which stands out in my memory.

As a student on Tresco one of the highlights of the practical year has to be the clipping of the high evergreen oak hedges. From January through to March this collection of trees are trimmed before the arrival of the visitors. Standing up to 10.5m (35ft) tall in some cases, a head for heights is needed for the ladderwork involved. Two persons at any one time work as a team, alternating between being at the top of ladder and ground man or woman.

Once into the second part of the year each student is required to conduct guided tours of the garden to visiting

Below: Show material ready for dispatch on Carn Near Quay.

60

Right: The Old Abbey. (Frank Naylor

groups. There is always a look of horror when this is first suggested but we find that in a very short space of time, all students develop great confidence and style. The history of the development of the garden, plant content and island life are all included in the garden stroll. Each party is met from the helicopter or boat and at the end of the tour shown the delights of the Garden Shop and Cafe in case they wish to purchase a tasteful gift or sample a piping hot sausage roll, washed down by scalding, but well-priced, tea!

Passenger cruise ships are regular visitors to the islands and some summer seasons will see up to twenty-five vessels making calls. Most are making circular tours around the coast of Britain or returning to and from the Mediterranean. It is not unusual to be confronted by three hundred and fifty passengers eager to see the garden at the same time. They are divided into more manageable groups of around thirty between students and gardeners alike. The next trick is to avoid other groups when moving about the garden. If two groups meet on a small path it can resemble Oxford Street in the January sales! It has also been known for the odd ship to leave passengers behind on Tresco and to sail off into the sunset (literally)! Overnight stays and flights are then organised for the bereft passenger to catch the ship at the next port. It can be a lot of fun!

When living on a small island with a small population, community affairs will always play a big part in our lives and students are encouraged to join in the everyday activities. Sport, if the student is so inclined, plays a large role in his/her off-duty time. There is badminton and table tennis in the winter and tennis, sailing, windsurfing, gig rowing and cricket in the summer. Alasdair Moore our student 1992-93 joined us from the Royal Parks of London and was a keen and able cricketer. Within two weeks of his arrival on the island he was at the crease batting for the Tresco Eleven, when a fine edge off his bat found the ball glancing off his head causing a nasty cut. A tractor ride to the quay and a fast boat to St Mary's saw Alasdair to the hospital. Five stitches later and the boat and tractor in reverse order, saw him finish the game taking two wickets for no runs in the final over. We were impressed!

Gig rowing is the major sport on Scilly from April to October. Pilot gigs were used in the past to ferry pilots out to waiting ships needing guidance through or into the islands. Long wooden craft, gigs are rowed by six oars and a coxswain. Every Friday (men) and Wednesday (ladies) they are raced from different points around the islands. At least eight boats take part in races up to three miles long. Gardeners and students alike have rowed for many years for Tresco and Bryher Rowing Club in these epic battles. Many

a Monday morning garden tea-break has turned into a debate on the merits of thirty strokes a minute or the lack of effort by the bow paddle. It is not for the faint hearted and when interviews take place in London you cannot help but size someone up as a possible strong oar. Ex-students Alison Smith 1997-98 and Alison Read 1998-99 are two who have distinguished themselves in the heat of battle for the ladies' crews.

During the summer months Tresco seems to have an inordinate number of fetes. Our garden students are usually enrolled to supervise the obligatory plant stand provided as usual by the propagating department and will be dragged kicking and screaming to the allotted area in some deserted corner of an overgrown field known as the village green, where they are forced to smile and take money from holidaymakers in return for assorted garden leftovers.

Many ex-Studley/Tresco students now manage Cornish gardens of their own. Rachel Martin (Tresco 1994-95) has since become head gardener at Trebah, the garden so much brought back to life by Major Tony Hibbert. John Lanyon (Tresco 1984-85) - he of the tree climbing exploits - is now the National Trust head gardener at Cotehele House near Saltash. Ian Wright (Tresco 1983-84) has been head gardener for the National Trust at The Vyne, Hampshire for many years. Stephen Crisp (Tresco 1979) has a more cosmopolitan outlook on life and has been in control of matters horticultural, both indoors and out, at the London residence of the United States Ambassador.

Left: The Succulent Rockery. (Derek Harris)

62

Right: The Middle Terrace. (Derek Harris)

64

*Right: Villa
Orengo The
Hanbury Garden,
La Mortola.
Gardeners' visit
1999.*

THE WIDER WORLD

Because of Tresco's reputation it has never been difficult to attract both new plants and new visitors. Collecting plants and making new contacts in a garden such as ours can be therefore sometimes taken for granted. New ideas are always needed to inject fresh life and enthusiasm into both gardeners and gardens.

We had wished for some time to establish links with European gardens with similar plant collections, to look at different species and to compare working practice, garden design and, very importantly, to exchange plants and if possible gardeners.

Since my student days one garden had always held me in its spell: a fabulous garden planted by a family on the French/Italian border on the coast between Nice and the small Italian town of Ventimiglia: The Hanbury Garden at La Mortola. Since taking over at Tresco it had always been an ambition of mine to forge some sort of link between both gardens, so when I was approached in the spring of 1996 by Simon Hanbury, at the time the current member of the Hanbury family in residence at La Mortola, with a proposal for an informal 'twinning' between the gardens, I was delighted. It became clear very quickly that we both wished to follow the same route in terms of staff exchange, plant and seed movement.

The opportunity for a complete garden staff to be absent is not the easiest thing to organise but in February 1999 seven members of our gardening team departed from Tresco for the French /Italian Riviera. Festooned with extra garden tools, secateurs plant labels, notebooks, French francs, Italian lire and suntan lotion we set off.

The garden at La Mortola was purchased in 1867 by Sir Thomas Hanbury who with the help of his brother, Daniel, created one of the most renowned collections of plants in the world. The gardens extend onto a southern sloped promontory from the village of La Mortola dropping sharply 100m (300ft) down to the sea's edge. The microclimate is unusual due to its optimum southern exposure, and the peaks of the Bellenda and Magliocca Mountains provide shelter from the north and northwesterly winds.

By 1912 the family had collected over six thousand specimens and this continued to be expanded by successive generations. Dorothy Hanbury ran the garden until 1960 but ill health and shortage of money caused the sale of the garden to the Italian government. A period of semi-neglect ensued until 1987 when the garden was handed over to the University of Genoa. It is now open to the public all year round and a plan to restore the garden to full glory is well under way. The garden currently has twelve gardeners who are spread about the 18 hectares. Each gardener is responsible for a set area and groups of plants within that area. The garden is a plantsman's paradise with many botanical collections such as palms, aloes, succulents, fruits, cycads, conifers and cacti.

It was fascinating to see how the difference in climate affected the two Mediterranean collections at Tresco and the Hanbury. The very hot summer temperatures on the Italian coast ensured that all the climbing plants flowered very strongly, whilst on Tresco they produce abundant foliage but little flower. Equally, because of mild winters, Proteacea flower strongly on Tresco and are well represented, while at the Hanbury they are not so successful.

We spent our mornings in the garden on particular assignments, taking cuttings and gathering seedling plants, which are now planted in an area below the Pebble Garden on Tresco and the afternoons visiting other local gardens to see what we could learn. We visited the garden of the Villa Val Rahmeh, which has for many years produced an Index Seminum, an annual seed exchange list passed out to botanic and other interested gardens. Seeing the plants in situ

Left: William Waterfield in his garden at Clos du Peyronnet. Gardeners' visit 1999.

makes a big difference to future requests as we have a better understanding of the growing conditions

We also visited the garden begun by Major Lawrence Johnston (of Hidcote Manor fame) in the nearby Gorbio Valley above Menton in the early 1920s and the garden of William Waterfield, Clos du Peyronnet, at Menton-Garavan close to the French/Italian border, where his own collection of over two hundred species of bulbs are displayed in a special corner. The visit to Les Columbières showed us how landscape can be used within a garden.

We went to Villa Les Cedres on Cap Ferrat to see the collections held in a range of twenty-two glasshouses that would rival any national botanic garden. Here Rene Hebding the curator of twenty years standing escorted us. He had devoted his day to us, pointing out many hundreds of plants, and we filled many notebooks with his detailed information. We also enjoyed the Exotic Garden at Monte Carlo, which specialises in cacti and succulents. Tresco has been in contact with the Exotic for many years in a small way in the form of seed exchange lists. To visit and see for ourselves the 'backroom' operation has opened up a whole new avenue for us to explore.

The informal discussions between gardeners and curators, the exchange of information and plants or seeds and the viewing of growing conditions on site are invaluable to the development and growth of the Abbey Garden. We are grateful for the opportunity to do so. It is hoped that these links can be maintained and future exchanges can be arranged.

Right: Abbey Gardeners in The Hanbury admiring the South African Aloes. 1999.

Far left:
Mid-garden view
Tresco.

*Left: Mid-garden
view. The Hanbury
Garden - spot the
difference!*

THE SNOW 1987

I t could be said that at some point in a gardener's life he or she will be presented with a challenge. Our challenge came in January 1987 in the form of snow, ice and freezing temperatures.

Because of the Gulf Stream the temperature of the garden very rarely drops below 10C. On one afternoon in January 1987 a heavy snowfall descended upon the garden very quickly, giving the gardeners little time to prepare for what was to dominate their working lives for the next ten years.

As the snow fell we moved about the garden armed with rakes, knocking and brushing large drifts from weighed, down branches. The sound of breaking boughs indicated the severity and volume of the snowfall. After a very short time and a very uneven battle we gave up and took to toboggan rides perched on fertiliser bags on some of the more precipitous garden slopes. As supposedly mature adults we assumed the snow was to be nothing more than an inconvenience and we took advantage in a playful way.

However, the temperature soon dropped to -8C and this, coupled with a 25 knot easterly wind, took the wind chill factor down to between -25/30C. Over the next fifteen days the snows gradually receded but the temperatures remained the same. Up to this point our only worry had been for the plants sat above the snow in the biting winds. The real problem came for the many thousands of tender plants now exposed by the destruction of their natural shelter to the ferocious gales coupled with the massive drop in temperature.

Our immediate concerns were proved correct when before our eyes the garden appeared to be falling to pieces as succulent exotics rotted, dripped and collapsed into oblivion. Large clump-forming South African Aloes of up to 6 - 9m (20 - 30ft) across fell into tangled heaps, the water-filled trunks frozen to death. Palm trees of over fifty years old such as the Nikau Palm *Rhopalostylis sapida* completely lost their growing centres and bucket-loads of what looked like stewed rhubarb, and smelt like something far worse, fell apart at ground level. Canary Island Echium shrubs gradually dropped first their leaves and then their branches in a slow and painful effort to stay alive. This was to be the pattern over the next few weeks and months with 80% of the garden specimens being affected. Each plant family appeared to have its own time scale in which it clung to life until no longer able to survive.

At first our reaction was one of disbelief. Certainly in the previous 150 years extreme weather conditions had caused considerable damage in the garden - but this was on a scale never previously recorded.

The garden had matured over many years to produce magnificent individual specimens: for example the frost-tender New Zealand Flame Trees introduced in 1851. These grand old men of the garden, with a height of some 18 - 21m (60 - 70ft) and girth up to 6m (20ft) around, started to drop their leaves. Because they are evergreen we knew that for these trees to show such a sign was deadly serious. Over the next months all the flame trees, without exception, lost every leaf, appearing like skeletal sculptures placed about the garden as if on exhibition.

Similar havoc was wrought across the garden throughout the early spring and summer until we found ourselves in the bizarre situation of calling ourselves a garden but with nothing that resembled a garden to show for it.

Pitiful attempts to add colourful summer bedding schemes as some sort of compensation to the horticulturally deprived public fell flat. Small patches of colour amongst the dead and dying failed to make any impact. Hurried but considered notices were erected both inside and outside the garden explaining the ghastly predicament in which we found ourselves. Our plea was for visitors to continue to visit and

Above: **Phoenix canariensis** *and* **Agave americana** *subdued by the snow. (Robert A.Dorrien-Smith)*

Far left: The snows across to Bryher.

70

Right: Snow, the secret destroyer.

Below: The Old Abbey under snow, January 1987. (Robert A. Dorrien-Smith)

pay the much needed entry fee which would allow the garden to carry on with some sort of normality even though we knew everything was far from normal. We can look back and honestly say the reaction from the visiting public was in every way sympathetic and supportive and this gave us great heart in our work.

Ex-garden staff of many years experience had seen nothing like it in the whole of their careers whilst on Tresco. To see their lifetimes' work destroyed was very hard for them to take. In many cases we drew upon their experience with some of the practical tasks of pruning and cutting back in a vain attempt to halt the destruction. In a normal gardening year the spring months mean extra work and a busy growing and planting period, now the tasks of removing and digging out old favourites within the garden became heartbreaking. One particular tree that had become a great favourite over the years with regular garden visitors was *Araucaria excelsa*, otherwise known as the Norfolk Island Pine. Standing at over 22.5m (75ft) high, this tree had now died standing up. Rather than just cut it off at ground level we had to excavate all roots to be able to give us the chance of replanting a fresh specimen in its place. Many days' work followed in the removal firstly of large quantities of soil and then the back-breaking spadework necessary to break up the root system for removal. The rootball was removed to a nearby path by some very impressive winch manoeuvres, only for us to discover it was far too large to take away. Being a small island with not a great deal of heavy plant machinery and also being a garden that had only small paths it meant there was only one possible solution - dynamite!

A local diver from Bryher was called in to assist in resolving our knotty problem. The garden was closed to the general public for obvious safety reasons and the scene was set. Our explosives expert set the charges, gardeners were placed in safe areas, whistles were blown and a very loud noise followed. We rushed across to inspect our handiwork to find the root had split very neatly in two - mission accomplished. This fired our enthusiasm for future explosive exploits and our root removing troubles were over, or so we thought!

The next project involved a large palm specimen that needed removing from the main garden walk situated not far from the entrance. The same procedure followed, charges set, whistles, loud bang; on inspection we found a very neat hole in the ground but no sign of the offending stump. I have neglected to mention that rather than bother with the tedious process of removing or loosening the stump we went for a straight forward explosive extraction -

Top: Evergreen metrosideros, the New Zealand Flame Tree. (Frank Naylor)

Middle: Spring 1988: skeletal form.

Bottom: Spring 1989: cut back to ground level to stimulate regrowth.

not a good idea! Apart from a huge shower of soil, which had to be raked up, of the stump there was no sign. Further inquiries showed that the stump had taken flight in an upward direction, flown over a substantial area of the garden to deposit itself very neatly next to the potting shed door. Andrew Lawson, hearing a dull thud came out of the shed to find a substantial 34-kilo (75lb) palm stump outside. By coincidence we found some three weeks later that an adjacent wall had collapsed - we never found out why! This episode, one of many that involved explosives, led us back to the more traditional methods of stump removal. Where did we put those spades?

To say the gardeners worked hard in that period would be a gross understatement. With Robert Dorrien-Smith's very considerable encouragement and support the entire team was able to cast aside any negative thoughts. Sleeves were simply rolled up to get the job done.

Beside the concern about the plants themselves we still had many garden visitors whose safety had to be considered. Many of the more woody specimens of any size such as the New Zealand Flame Trees had began to drop substantial sections of branches, usually in gales but also in completely calm weather. This does not go down well if

Far left: Norfolk Island Pine, 27m (90ft) tall killed standing 1987.

Left: Spring 1988, digging the rootplate to remove the tree. Steve Parkes, Andrew Lawson and Frank Naylor.

Below left: The gardeners drilling the stump prior to dynamiting!

Below: January 1987, **Phoenix canariensis** *with snow damage.*

Right: Total recovery.

74

you are a member of the paying public. It is always nice to get close to the plants in a garden, but not that close, especially if it happens to drop from 12m (40ft) up. Much vigorous tree surgery therefore took place about the garden, each tree needing different consideration and treatment depending on age and size.

Andrew Lawson, the present head gardener, and myself were the two most experienced tree surgeons. We approached the high climbing work with ropes, harness and chainsaws. Many of the trees needed to be cut at a point where we assumed that regeneration would occur, so in many cases it would take more than one attempt before the right height was found. We were working blind so to speak with no previous experience or knowledge of how these particular trees were going to respond, in the long term, to the freezing conditions they had experienced. It would be a case of cut it down, wait a bit, and cut off a bit more.

Top right: June/July 1987. South Africa Cliff bereft of plants. 18m (60ft) high evergreen **Banksia integrifolia** *dying.*

Right: Spring 1988. Dead and dangerous branches have been cut from the Banksia, bringing it to ground level

It is a fairly exhausting process spending a complete day spinning about the crown of a tree, cutting, lowering and trying, on odd occasions, to kill your ground man with out-of-control branches! The occasional thermos flask, sandwich and cake would ascend on the ropes to give sustenance and energy, as lunch would be taken up above rather than waste valuable time pulling each other up and down uncomfortable and awkward trunks.

Over the spring and summer months this arboricultural slaughter was repeated time and time again right across the garden and had the effect of opening areas to the wind and creating much higher light levels. The accumulated weed seeds quickly germinated in these favourable conditions with little or no competition from garden ornamentals, which meant vast tracts of ground were covered with pernicious weed. The delightful process of weeding was very much disliked by the gardeners and the tedious removal of these weeds became a daily ritual, although we had very little to show for our efforts.

At the end of a very exhausting season, both mentally and physically, it was decided to begin the Herculean process of restocking. Our own glasshouse range was sufficient only to maintain a modest collection. We needed therefore to travel further afield to replace many hundreds of lost and damaged plant species.

Complete collections and groups of plants had perished: Aeonium from the Canary Islands, Protea and Leucadendron from the South African Cape, Acacia from Australia and Leptospermum from New Zealand to name but a few. Throughout the year copious notes had been taken recording the different and varied ways the plant life had responded in vain attempts at regeneration - if indeed there had been any at all.

The first priority was to replace many of the established plant groups lost. This did not mean there would be no room for fresh new species, far from it. But in a practical sense we could not sit about for too long. The garden needed to be replenished and quickly. The collection on Tresco is so complex and unique that we knew our search for plants would take us far and wide.

Right: The Succulent Rockery. (Derek Harris)

PLANT COLLECTING

A hunting we will go

In the October of 1987 Andrew Lawson and I set off on the first of what would become numerous collecting excursions gathering plant material to replace what had been lost. This inaugural trip started on the quay at New Grimsby, Tresco, at 6.30 am on a cold and damp morning in thick fog. After a day's delay we were able to set forth. By the time we had reached the Scottish borders that first evening our lorry driving skills had improved ten-fold as Andrew and I settled for a supper of haggis and chips before looking for a hotel for the night.

Our destination was the Logan Botanical Garden in Scotland which is an annexe of the Royal Botanic Garden, Edinburgh. It is situated fourteen miles south of Stranraer, midway down the narrow peninsular of the Mull of Galloway. I had written to Barry Unwin, the garden assistant curator, explaining our problems and he had kindly made plant material available. Logan has a very similar climate to Tresco with perhaps double the rainfall (our rainfall is 30 inches per year). Due to the higher rainfall, Logan holds many specimens from New Zealand, such as the tree ferns which had been lost to Tresco. *Dicksonia antarctica* and *Cyathea medullaris* had been introduced to Tresco as early as 1851 and had over the 140 years grown in some cases to well over five metres - these were obviously important in terms of replacement. Many shrub *Olearia* species and cultivars that needed replacing at Tresco were also made available in the form of small plants or cutting material along with a collection of Salvia cuttings.

One of the huge advantages of this particular trip around a collection of British gardens had been the anticipation of visiting for either the first time, or revisiting of gardens after many years, and pulling on the knowledge and expertise of various friends and colleagues. Amenity horticulture has always in my experience been a welcoming and giving profession. After the summer of misery watching Tresco fall to pieces, meeting up with fresh faces full of enthusiasm made a big difference to Andrew and myself in terms of morale. This first port of call at Logan really felt like the start of the new beginning for the garden and us.

If we thought that Logan felt a long way from Scilly, then our next visit took us further north and west to the village of Poolewe, Ross and Cromarty, in the Highlands. Our destination was the Scottish National Trust garden at Inverewe. We had arranged to stay midpoint between Logan and Inverewe at a friend and colleague's house on the banks of Loch Lomond. Maurice Wilkins was head gardener at Ross Priory: a garden attached to the University of Strathclyde. Maurice and I had met many years previously and kept in regular touch through meetings of The Professional Gardeners' Guild. As is the custom among visiting gardeners, on arrival at his garden at Loch Lomond we took the 'five-shilling' tour with Maurice.

Our journey the next day started, as they seem to do on these occasions, at dawn. Having gone through the toast and two pots of tea, we started to say our goodbyes when Maurice inquired if we had room for a small one in the lorry. We assured him we did. At this point he called to his wife Sheila and told her he would be back in three days. What an understanding wife! Three or four hours into the day Maurice suggested an alternative route to the nice, wide main roads that so far had not failed us. As the local man Maurice told us we could not come all this way without driving through the Torridan Gap and one of the highlights of a Scottish tour. How could we refuse?

Admittedly the view had its finer points, but it began to lose its charm when we had to edge the lorry along a single track fit only for a fair sized pram. On we travelled until mid-afternoon found us on the outskirts of Poolewe: our

Far left: Another consignment from Kew being unloaded mid-channel between Tresco and Bryher. (Frank Gibson)

Above: Puya alpestris. (Andrew Lawson)

82

destination. We had expected a quiet village that day, instead we discovered that we had timed our arrival to coincide with the finish of the annual Poolewe Duck Race (plastic yellow ones, like you see in the bath). Not for us the peaceful sea loch, but five hundred ducks and five hundred cheering participants all willing on their own particular duck - of course, all perfectly normal in this part of the world. Passing on through this sporting extravaganza we arrived at the gates of Inverewe Gardens.

I had two very good reasons for wanting to visit this garden, not just for the plant collection but also for the man responsible for them at this time, Peter Clough. I had worked under Peter when I was a student on Tresco and his knowledge and enthusiasm were in my opinion second-

Above: Peter Clough in Inverewe Garden.

Right: Inverewe. The Tresco bandwagon rolls on!

Left: Lower Middle Terrace. (Simon McBride)

Above: Inverewe. Peter Clough, Andrew Lawson and Maurice Wilkins forage for material.

Right: Ron Gleadle filling the Scillonian container with plants donated by the Royal Botanic Garden, Kew.

to-none in the plant world. Beside the plant material we had come to collect, it was a chance to exchange views with Peter on the direction our work should take on Tresco. Over the course of the next two days we moved about Inverewe gardens and grounds extracting, not just plant material, but ideas and views on our course of action over the coming months back in Tresco Abbey Garden - discussion that proved to be immensely valuable. Meanwhile Maurice had collected his own small lorry-load of plants and cuttings, which needed to be transported back to his abandoned wife and children.

Peter's own brand of enthusiasm and optimism very quickly rubbed off on both Andrew and myself and by the end of our short stay we had a much clearer idea of how to tackle the immense task that lay ahead of us.

Our next appointment was at the Royal Botanic Garden, Edinburgh. Our contact was Ross Kirby, one of the garden curators, who was responsible for tender plants held at the garden. I had telephoned him earlier in the year and he had produced an impressive list of appropriate plants for us from the extensive collections held under glass. Our main objective was to replace plants, but here in Edinburgh, and later at the Royal Botanic Gardens at Kew, we were able to add new and exciting species to our collection.

We were given many plants from the frameyards and nurseries at Edinburgh, some familiar and others more interestingly unfamiliar - such unknown names (to me) as *Vernonia stenostegia*, a perennial herb from Nigeria. Also amidst the cutting material presented was a collection of South African Aloes of up to twenty-five different species. This was exactly the sort of material we had hoped for but never in reality had expected to be given. As our vehicle was filling, compulsory stops became necessary, not just to fuel, but to water our precious cargo. Andrew at various points disappeared into the darkest depths of our transport clutching a hosepipe normally reserved for the car wash. I then followed behind, repositioning any labels that had been lost from pots as a consequence of our driving skills.

Our next stop, after Edinburgh was Harewood House, just outside Harrogate, the site for many scenes in the television series 'Brideshead Revisited'. We had received a kind invitation from the then garden manager/ head gardener Alan Mason who I had first met, yet again through Professional Gardeners' Guild meetings.

Having heard of our horticultural plight, Alan provided a small but significant collection of semi-tender plants from his collections held under glass. From his peach house came such delights as *Clethra alnifolia* "Rosea" and *Helichrysum petiolatum* "Limelight", both of which now thrive on Tresco.

Continuing south we descended into deepest Suffolk to Talbot Manor. Robert Dorrien-Smith had been approached by Maurice Mason, a member of the Council of the Royal Horticultural Society, who had been a friend of Robert's father, Commander Tom Dorrien-Smith, and like many others had made an offer of plant material. Over many years, Maurice Mason had built up a private collection of tender plants to rival any botanic garden. All were held under glass, very well labelled and benefiting from the full time care of two gardeners. Under the watchful, but generous, eye of head gardener Derek Kemp, Andrew and I took many hundreds of cuttings.

Of particular interest were the aloes from South Africa. Aloes are divided into many different groups such as tree, single-stemmed, multi-stemmed, creeping, stemless, speckled, spotted, dwarf and last, but not least, grass aloes. In South Africa alone there are one hundred and twenty-five species. Maurice Mason appeared to have most of them hidden amongst his varied and wide ranging collections. Canary Island *Aeonium tabulaeforme*, a succulent with the appearance of a plate, flat and circular, was collected as both plant and seed, a very prized specimen and something that had always grown well on Tresco. Two species of *Puya* from Chile were added to our haul. Puya are a group that has, even among the Tresco plant collection, stood out. Most puya

Left: Mike Nelhams selecting new plants at a garden nursery, Ventimiglia, Italy.

produce very showy and fast-growing flower-spikes in the early summer. In the wild humming birds will pollinate the plants, flying between flower stems, drinking nectar and transferring pollen as they go. On Tresco starlings and blackbirds achieve the same result, much to the delight of the visitors, as they see the birds move about, heads covered in bright orange pollen.

Ten years later, in 1997, Andrew and I made the trip back to Suffolk at the invitation of Hugh Mason. Hugh was in the process of re-siting his father's old collection to new premises. He had phoned to offer Tresco first pick of the surplus before closing down the old glasshouse range built by his father. We arrived to be met as before by Derek Kemp, still in command of the collection and overseeing the enormous move. The old wooden houses were to be replaced by a modern aluminium range two miles down the road at an area behind Hugh's house. His intention was to also create an arboretum with the tender plants as the focal point. On the day of our arrival an extremely savage and strong wind was howling across the flatlands, which from what I could see, consisted mainly of swede crops, which gave the new range of glasshouses no protection whatsoever. Inside the new houses there was a distinct feeling that at any moment the whole structure would take off and land in the next field. I can only hope that they are still there in one piece. Everyone was more than generous in the amount and range of material offered and a wonderful example of the kindness shown by the gardening world.

Our British tour was coming to an end, but not before the grand finale, a visit to the Royal Botanic Gardens, Kew. We had made arrangements to descend upon the supervisors of both the Tropical and Temperate Nurseries. The plants available to us had been circulated earlier in the year as surplus to requirements at Kew. I had sweated over many textbooks in the previous months putting in bids for plants familiar and unfamiliar.

The Temperate Department grows particularly for siting in the main Temperate House at Kew, which represents the mainly Mediterranean regions of the world. During the year surplus plant lists are circulated to botanic gardens and gardens such as Tresco. Kew sends out plant collectors all over the world. Seed is returned to Kew for germination, distribution or research. A certain amount of seed will be sown for use at Kew but often there is a surplus. These collecting trips are therefore of great benefit to both Kew and the recipient garden. If for some reason disease, disorder or pest damage kills the plant in situ, then Kew can go back to the garden and reclaim material or seed, confident that the material has a known history.

Top right: Plants from collecting trips safely installed in the Tresco glasshouses.

Right: Three years on the garden returns. Mike Nelhams and Frank Naylor.

We were very fortunate to be able to tap into such a
rich source of the right material. Kew has undoubtedly
been a major factor in the revival of Tresco Abbey Garden.
Martin Staniforth was, and still is, Nursery supervisor at the
Temperate Nursery. He and a member of his team, John
Sitch, were ready and waiting with our allocated plant
material. We had not prepared ourselves for the range or
size of many plants waiting to be shipped. A 3m (9ft) tall
Knightia excelsa, the New Zealand honeysuckle tree in the
Proteaceae family, immediately comes to mind when recall-
ing loading our already bursting-at-the-seams vehicle. There

*Above: Planting
the spoils.*

was also, from the arid Australian regions, the wonderfully named *Hakea epiglottis*, a small white flowered shrub that would be ideal for the Top Terrace on Tresco, and *Canarina canariensis*, the Canary Island bellflower, a climber and rambler decorated with orange/yellow striped pendulous flowers. Each new plant excited us and as we loaded, mental notes were taken for a planting position in the garden on our return.

Not just on this particular trip but on many subsequent occasions over the next five years, Kew Gardens staff, particularly Mark Sparrow, supervisor of the Temperate House and David Cooke, a Supervisor in the Palm House, provided an enormous range of plants which formed the basis of the recovery of Tresco Abbey Garden.

My regular visits from 1987 have enabled me to take a different member of staff from Tresco to assist me. This is useful both practically and educationally as it illustrates clearly to each gardener how these plants come to be making their way to us. On one memorable occasion we were contacted by the Palm House asking if we would be interested in trying out a palm from the Canary Islands. We said of course we would and were then informed that this particular specimen weighed half a ton - with pot! We duly arrived at Kew on the appointed day driving through the garden via a network of paths to the doors of the Palm House. With help from members of the Kew staff and forklift trucks the palm was deposited, with much pushing, panting and the occasional trapped finger, into our lorry.

During this period of frantic collecting I was asked to lecture to the Kew Mutual Society. Through the winter months a series of lectures are given by both in-house and outside speakers at the Joderell Lecture hall at Kew. My subject was, as you may imagine, Tresco and the hoped-for revival of the garden. Through quivering voice and an assortment of nervous twitches I managed to recount the garden history, to tell of the commitment of the Dorrien-Smith family, to describe the plant collections and give an update on the current situation. It was very pleasing for me, on behalf of Tresco, to be able to thank Kew for the unstinting help and co-operation we had been given during that difficult time. At the end of the lecture Kew presented Tresco with a specimen of *Meryta sinclairii*, a handsome tree from Three Kings Island in the Pacific. Before the big freeze of 1987 this had been one of our garden's prized specimens. The plant now sits in an area in the centre of the garden and is thriving. From the director and curator, through to the freshest of the students, the enthusiasm and willingness to assist us always made our trips to Kew something to enjoy and to be grateful for.

Far left: Mexican Agave. (Jerry Harpur)

Left: **Leucospermum tottum**. *(Andrew Lawson)*

Right: The Middle
Terrace.
(Jerry Harpur)

Many other gardens have made major contributions and cannot be forgotten. Sutton Place, Surrey, the old home of millionaire Paul Getty; Somerset College of Horticulture, Cannington; Bristol University; the Chelsea Physic Garden, London; Abbotsbury in Dorset; Ventnor Botanic Garden on the Isle of Wight; Knightshayes Court, Devon; Savill Garden, Windsor; R.H.S. Wisley; R.H.S. Rosemoor and of course a full set of the Cornish gardens: St Michael's Mount, Trengwainton, Tregrehan, Trebah, Carwinnion, Fox Rosehill Falmouth Parks, Lanhydrock, Trelissick, Trewidden, Trewithen, Tregothnan and many individual small private gardens across the county.

Getting the plants back to Tresco was quite an undertaking. On arrival at Penzance Docks all plants were removed from the lorries and placed in ship's containers for the voyage to Scilly. Each container was packed as tightly as possible to aid safe arrival and then loaded aboard in Penzance for the short trip to St Mary's. From there a smaller boat brought our prize cargo to one of three quays on Tresco depending on the state of the tide. On many occasions this meant removal from the container at the quay and transfer into assorted tractors and trailers for the drive to the garden. Finally each plant, labelled, catalogued and watered found its way into the small glasshouse range. Every specimen was then, depending on size, condition and age, potted, had cuttings taken or planted in the garden. Having gone through the collecting and gathering there is nothing more pleasurable than siting and planting. Knowing where and from whom the plant has come, with the work involved, adds greatly to the satisfaction. Not all planting however succeeds and many new and untried plants fail because of weather, poor siting and our lack of knowledge. It can be infuriating when having researched a plant you feel it should do well but it resists all attempts to grow; that is the luck of the draw; we can but try again. Since 1987 this process of gathering and restocking has been continuing in what we hope is a fairly orderly fashion.

Our aim to build up collections in this manner appeared to be working. From January 1987 to October 1990 planting within the garden took place at a rate previously unseen. Our monthly temperatures meant that we were able to plant at almost any time of the year. We devised a planting policy that took into account whole plant collections rather than random plantings. Each group was gathered together by seeding, growing cuttings or by collecting from gardens and nurseries before being planted en masse. Large groups of Protea, Banksia, Aeonium, Aloe, Acacia, Lampranthus, Echium, along with smaller numbers of genus and species, had begun to form the backbone of our plans.

Our planting positions for each genus used past experience and the knowledge gained from the previous 150 years of the garden as well as our own personal views. The natural aspect of the garden, a south facing slope on a hillside, meant that we have a natural order in our plantings. The top terrace with its poor shallow soil in combination with lack of shade has always adapted well to plants from South Africa/Australia and Mexico. The Middle Terrace with slightly deeper soil and slightly more protected from the gales has the look of the French Rivera, with many plants also coming from the Canary Isles. Meanwhile the lower area sometimes gives the impression of being a typical Cornish garden trying to escape into the slightly exotic.

We took much advice from retired gardeners Frank Naylor and David Hopkins who between them had worked well over eighty years in the garden, thirty of them together, covering a period starting in 1934 and finishing in 1985. By 1990 things were looking up as the plantings and garden blossomed at a prodigious rate.

Left: **Banksia baxterii.**
(Andrew Lawson)

HURRICANE 1990

What have we done to deserve this?

If the sun is shining and the weather conditions mild it is very easy to imagine that all is well with the world, especially if your garden is recovering from the worst possible disaster in its history.

Things were going well in the Abbey Garden. Most of the visible signs of decay from the previous three years had been removed and our new planting schemes and introductions had at last begun to show signs of maturity. Admittedly many areas were sparsely populated but that is only to be expected when eighty per cent of the garden had been lost.

Walking into work from home on the morning of the 25th January 1990 gardener David Inch and I remarked that the wind was 'getting up' as they say in Cornwall. At that point we had absolutely no inkling of what was in store. This was at 8.00 am; by 9.00 am I had withdrawn all the gardeners from the grounds and had closeted them in the tool shed for safety. Andrew Lawson, Richard Hobbs and I decided to amuse ourselves with a visit to the 'seaside' to look at the waves. What was normally a two-minute walk became a ten-minute battle against an ever-increasing wind. Pushing in from a south-westerly direction the sea had become a boiling torrent between the islands. Waves were smashing onto the beaches and sea-defence walls, salt spray, an absolute menace to plant foliage, was being picked up and dumped on the garden by the bucketful, the wind carrying it some two or three hundred metres. Above the howling wind the sound of falling trees could be heard, first the thud, then the breaking branches smashing to the floor.

On our walk back to the garden - going with the wind rather more quickly than against it - we could see many gaps beginning to appear in our outer shelterbelts. Trees mainly consisting of the one hundred and thirty year-old Monterey pine, *Pinus radiata* and the Monterey cypress, *Cupressus macrocarpa*, from California, formed the backbone of our protective treeline. At this point, at roughly nine-thirty in the morning, the wind speed had picked up to 127 miles per hour which on the Beaufort scale is well into hurricane force.

Arriving back at the garden office I was given the message that my wife, Isobel, had called to say our house was being surrounded by falling trees. Our house at that time was on the fringe of woodland. The trees, all *Pinus radiata* and well into old age were well over 21 - 24.5m (70 - 80 ft) tall, top heavy - and big enough to crush the house if it hit directly. The island heliport manager and I went in the fire engine as far as possible until we came upon fallen trees which blocked our path. A quick dash of two hundred metres revealed that the house was still intact but only just. The surrounding area was littered with a forest of tangled trunks and branches; indeed one specimen had completely covered the front of the house taking off, luckily, only a small section of the front porch. Isobel and I hurriedly carried our two daughters Maxine and Katie across the fields to the village, away from any falling trees. This meant clambering over back garden fences carrying the girls who at that time were only five and two years old.

Returning to the garden I was met by the sight of the largest tree in the garden lying on its side like a mortally wounded elephant. This single tree, by coincidence also a Monterey cypress, had presided over a section of garden in need of shade. Below its branches it had protected many plants from New Zealand, such as *Dicksonia antarctica* and *Cyathea medullaris*: both tree ferns that in the winter months demanded shelter from salt spray and wind and in the summer from the drying breeze and the sun's glare. This would now be missing. The rootplate that had lifted was up to 6m (20ft) high and sat exposing the shallow root system so typical of trees in Scilly. Falling onto a nearby lawn, the tree had punched a hole in our outer protection and the wind

Above: Monterey Cypress 30m (100ft), the tallest tree in the garden fallen to earth.

was taking full advantage, a withering and piercing gale pushing onto rare and tender shrubs in the garden terraces.

The worst was yet to come. Unbeknown to us ninety per cent of our entire 130 year-old shelterbelt had crashed to the ground. Tresco Abbey Garden had been surrounded for most of its existence with a warm blanket of shelter. The majority of these trees had grown up together, all planted in the 1870 to 1890 period. The whole ghastly process had taken only four hours to destroy a complete hillside and eight hundred mature trees. Everything had grown together and everything fell together. Within the garden itself, many fine specimens ranging from 24.5m (80ft) tall *Eucalyptus globulus*, the Tasmanian blue gum, to countless hundreds of smaller ornamental and specimen trees such as the prized silver tree from South Africa, *Leucadendron argenteum* were destroyed. Movement around the garden, other than on foot, was totally impossible and even then we had to clamber and climb over the broken trees. Without exception every path was blocked. Pathways had been ripped to pieces; what had been formal walks now resembled tattered jungles. Edging stones had been thrown aside in all directions as the trees had tumbled. What may have previously been a five-minute stroll on the flat took on all the rigours of an army assault course.

As the gardeners emerged from the safety of the potting shed to take in the horrors of the morning it became quickly apparent that nothing quite like this had happened before - apart from the snow of '87. What had we done to deserve two such disasters in such quick succession?

Plants that had been replanted to replace those lost in the big freeze had perished and been lost under tons of broken branches. The sheer scale of the impending clean up far outweighed anything we had done before because of the haphazard nature of hurricane damage. As we looked towards the upper terrace and the top of the garden, the task ahead grew tenfold. Our skyline had changed and been lowered by 24.5-27.5m (80-90ft). With the exception of one or two battered specimens the top plateau on the north hill had lost every tree. In addition to this the inner hillside on the west side had been given the same treatment - goodbye to eight hundred trees! The destruction on the hillside was on a much greater scale with larger trees and lifted rootplates the size of houses. Again a ten-minute walk across the hill this time took very nearly two hours struggling through the undergrowth.

In a strange way it was almost exhilarating to have witnessed the power of the wind. The initial minutes were feverish as we rushed and clambered with an almost child-like excitement to see the damage. This wore off very quickly as the enormity of the task ahead dawned upon us.

Our first priority had to be access. Close inspection of our arboricultural equipment revealed that we were sorely underpowered. Of course this hurricane of January 1990 had hit most of Southern England and many gardens and gardeners were in the same predicament. The clamour for tools would be a bit of a scramble if we left it too late. I was able to contact one of our regular suppliers and purchase, before he ran out of stock, three very large and shiny power saws at very great expense. They say size does not matter, but in this case it did. When faced with trees of a circumference reaching 6m (20ft) or more we could not start the clearance without good equipment.

Our garden team at the time numbered six, so in teams of two, tractors, trailers and saws were despatched to all main pathways to begin clearing. One good-sized tree weighs many tons. The excess soil would firstly have to be removed by spade, mattock, axe or crow bar and the root fingers cut back piece by piece until small enough to transport out to the fire. Each stump could take many days and still be abandoned until a future date. In many cases old stumps would be taken and buried in the sand dunes to help consolidation and reduce erosion.

In the larger open spaces mountainous fires were started which would burn for many weeks with the ever-increasing debris. In the wet weather through the early months of the year the fires simply smouldered, surrounded by lakes of water. Working conditions were thus not ideal but we had to begin somewhere.

The approach of March and April signalled the arrival of

Above: Abbey Hill: the clearance begins using imported heavy machinery.

Left: Richard Hobbs and Mark Pender taking a breather. Clearing paths was a priority.

the garden visitors. We had to provide some sort of garden for them - shades of '87! This gave rise to the slightly comical sight of us putting in summer bedding plants while seeming to ignore the vast areas of broken and fallen trees and the general turmoil.

The hillside was an altogether different problem. We had to decide on a long-term strategy that was both practical and cost effective. You need to remember Tresco is a private and family run island with limited resources. The cost in physical and financial terms of rebuilding the garden yet again would be very high indeed. The woodland and hillside shelterbelt is the single most important feature in terms of garden preservation and without it the garden could not exist with the collections in its present form. The sheer scale of the work ahead was absolutely staggering. What had been orderly woodland with clearly defined paths and tracks had completely disappeared. Trees planted over one hundred years ago had been knocked over like skittles.

After much consideration a five-year work plan was devised by Robert Dorrien-Smith and Steve Parkes, our resident forester and woodland manager. The area of devastation was divided up into five separate sections and a clearance and replanting programme devised. This by no means covered all of the areas that demanded our attention nor would it be completed within five years, but it made a healthy start. We contacted English Heritage and the Countryside Commission who both agreed to render financial assistance over the five-year period. English Heritage quite rightly asked that we carry out an historical research and a field survey of the garden given its importance within British horticulture. Beside the plants, historical features within the garden such as the terraces, the Pebble Garden, figureheads and assorted Roman altars needed to be recorded. English Heritage appreciated that the shelterbelts were essential for the long-term future of the garden.

Woodland clearance was to be carried out by mainland contractors under the

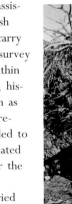

*Top: Aloe Walk before the hurricane. (Frank Naylor) Middle: Aloe Walk after the hurricane. The cordylines were especially difficult to grub out. Bottom: **Eucalyptus globulus** rootplate.*

supervision of Steve Parkes. An assortment of heavy machinery that included forestry grabs, winches, tractors and trailers was delivered to Penzance Docks for shipment over to the islands and then by an assortment of barges from St Mary's to Tresco.

The first hillside to be cleared was on the west side of the garden perimeter. On a fairly steep slope it represented at least one winter's work, cutting trunks, removing brushwood and replacing countless root plates and repairing the ground. Simply moving about quickly became a difficult task in a five-ton tractor on wet and boggy ground. Initially timber was removed, but soon bonfires resembling small volcanoes sprang up as a far quicker method of disposing of the increasing mountains of wood.

By the end of the first summer a semblance of order had returned to the garden. One area known as Long Walk had lost many large specimens with one big loss being a 21.5m (70ft) tall *Eucalyptus globulus* that had on its descent bundled over several other large trees. Even though the rootball was completely out of the ground on its edge, at the end of the summer months the stump was still attempting to produce growing tips. It was amazing to see such a tree struggling to survive.

Work now proceeded on the northern hill above the garden. The drier weather in the summer enabled us to remove wood from the site far more easily and familiarity with the equipment was also an important factor. All timber was transported to the dunes for storage in 3.5m (12ft) sections and stacked. Planting had already begun outside the remains of the original shelterbelts which increased the depth of tree cover while waiting for the remainder of the work to be completed. Within the garden what little remained standing was left and continued to be vital in sheltering the garden while we waited for our new planting to take effect. As a back-up lathe windbreaks were extensively used throughout the garden to replace or protect new plantings. Our records show as early as 1868 that similar sections were used in much the same way. By erecting poles and using two sections a height of

2.5-3m (8-10ft) could be achieved. Although not particularly beautiful they have proved to be remarkably effective.
Where possible, and in many cases, vigorous climbers such
as *Dolichos lignosus* and *Eleagnus reflexa* have been used to
shield the appearance of the fence while plants behind, or
indeed in front, grow to the required height. Creating a
network of smaller gardens by the use of the lathe sections
enabled the gardeners to focus their concentration on cultivation, planning, planting and landscaping in a particular
area rather than feel the garden was escaping them amidst
the turmoil.

The perimeter walls had suffered very badly as they had
been lifted by the rootplates, or trunks had broken them
down. This created the very large and real problem of rab-
bits infesting the garden. In the past the only creatures to
breach our walls had been geographically impaired holidaymakers unable to find a way into our garden other than
clambering over 2 metres of granite wall in an attempt to
find horticultural solace. Not for them the torture of the
garden entrance.

For that summer any spare time we had was spent
repairing walls and setting up wire netting fences. Our
thoughts now began to turn to the replanting and revival of
the shelterbelts, what species of plants should be used,
where we would obtain them and the husbandry and aftercare they would need once established.

*Top: After the
snow artificial
shelter had to be
erected. This
proved very
effective
Above right:
until...*

At the top of the list would of course be our reliable friends *Cupressus macrocarpa* and *Pinus radiata* from Monterey, California. Both were tried and tested, quick growing and wind and salt tolerant. Following closely behind were *Metrosideros excelsa* and *Metrosideros robusta* from New Zealand and, although both frost tender, they were by far the best at coping with strong winds but not so quick growing in the early years.

Within these belts many tender but sturdy species such as Eucalyptus from Australia, Araucaria from the Pacific Islands and *Clethra arborea* from Madeira which grows to well over 18m (60ft) high and is, as a bonus, covered in flowers in the autumn. As under-plantings to nurse the major shelter trees, *Olearia traversii* is always a first choice. Well known to Scillonian farmers as a hedge plant the Olearia makes a very handsome and fast growing shield for the young seedling evergreens. It comes from New Zealand and has silky white tomentose leaves and can grow to over 10m (34ft). *Pittosporum crassifolium*, *Griselinia littoralis* and the wonderfully named *Brachyglottis repanda* would also all play a part in early protection. All of these plants will grow very quickly in adverse conditions and protect the shelter trees until sturdy enough to fend for themselves.

Above: Frank Naylor and Mike Nelhams planting in front of the new shelterscreens 1992.

*Right: New plantings of **Cordyline albertii** within the garden.*

In the same way, as within the garden when light levels were raised, we knew many natural seedlings would emerge. Quite how many surprised even the Abbey gardeners! In the summer months of 1990 we often took time to botanise on the hillsides above the garden.

Major Arthur Dorrien-Smith and Commander Tom Dorrien-Smith had often initiated planting sprees within the shelterbelts with members of the family and guests staying on the island. To the different generations of the family it has always been considered that the hillside plays just as an important role as the garden proper. In a much more informal way the hill had a charm of its own and is quite unique in British horticulture. Space was freely available to plant groves of trees rather than one or two specimens. This often gave the impression of natural forest rather than managed woodland and was very pleasing to the eye. Plants and seed would be acquired in different ways. Much would come by the normal Botanic Garden route in seed exchange programmes. Members of the family visited gardens across the world bringing back seed to be grown on and planted.

Mrs Anne Philimore, daughter of Major A.A. Dorrien-Smith, devoted much of her time to the garden. She travelled far and wide as a member of the International Dendrology Society, (the scientific study of trees), visiting gardens and forest areas of many regions. On her return seed would be left with either the head gardener or propagator at the time. Perhaps six months later inquiries would be made of the progress of seed and readiness for planting. No slacking or forgetfulness was allowed and quite rightly so. Her suggestions for suitable planting positions were usually acted upon!

When plants were considered ready mini expeditions onto the hillside would be made with barrow-loads of plants. Organised by the leading family member, plants would be discussed, positioned and planted in great numbers. Some areas would be artificially screened as protection from unfriendly winds by erecting wire and hanging dead branches in a fence-like manner. Years later, when clearing, these were not so popular amongst the gardeners! Hitting a wire strut or cable with a chain saw was no joke! The range of plants used was quite staggering. Vast numbers of Australian acacia, from *Acacia melanoxylon* growing to a height of 21m (70ft), down to large sprawling bushes of *Acacia verticillata*, a rambling, crawling shrub that walks across the forest floor and can spread up to 15-18m (50-60ft) across or *Eucalyptus ficifolia*, a red flowering gum, which flowers in September on Tresco.

Extensive drifts of Leptospermum - the Australian tea tree - of many different kinds provided flower in the early

spring. Climbing Fuschia clambered through trees and the branches of evergreen oak and *Rhododendron ponticum*. *Banksia integrifolia*, again from Australia, and very much a prized specimen even in botanic gardens, could be found dotted along woodland path edges. Beneath the larger trees and in shady areas lurked the tree ferns from New Zealand and Tasmania. Alongside the tree ferns lived some of our favourite trees on Tresco the Kauri pines. There was also *Agathis australis*, which is normally only found in the Southern Hemisphere. These trees evolved in the Jurassic period some 150 million years ago. Agathis is a genus of some twenty large trees found mainly around the West Pacific, Australia, Indonesia and Fiji. Our one species however is only found in New Zealand.

Above: Anne Phillimore, daughter of The Major, a great lover of the garden.

Smaller and lower plants would inhabit the woodland floor. Carpets of a low shrub, *Correa backhousiana*, formed thickets, with each bush covered with small yellow tubular flowers. Standing out in lighter areas with more sunlight were *Pelargonium tomentosum*, a heavily peppermint scented low-growing plant from South Africa. The list is seemingly endless and these are just a fraction of the plants that make the hill so special.

All practical preparation towards planting and aftercare was carried out by Steve Parkes our woodland manager. It had been decided to use a mixture of plant sources. First stage plants were bought in from Duchy Woodland Nursery, Lostwithiel, Cornwall which would save valuable time while waiting for the Tresco seed to germinate. One extra advantage of the machinery trundling about on the hillsides when clearing felled trees was to mix up the soil layer and release oxygen and water which in turn assisted the growth of young trees. We also used one-year-old plants. Due to the shallow soil anything larger would not establish itself. Tree guards were used for all the new trees which were planted at a three-metre spacing. With small transplants the weed control needed to be efficient in and around the guards. Any competition for light would mean a wasted plant. It was soon discovered that with high light levels natural seedlings grew abundantly and soon overtook planned planting. Over a period of ten years one of the biggest advantages and disadvantages has been this over-growth. The advantage of natural seedlings is their vigour and stability. The very big drawback is the eventual over-crowding when re-spacing. In many areas thinning did not take place in time and natural tree shape was lost due to overcrowding - once the natural shape is gone it will rarely recover. We discovered by our own efforts that early spacing and thinning is the single most important fact when establishing an amenity woodland or shelterbelt.

Sixty thousand trees were planted, which has laid down a foundation for future gardeners to work on. We feel that overall it has been a great success and now, after ten years, the woodlands are starting to emerge from the under-growth. In only a very few years we shall have full protection from the Atlantic gales once more.

Right: Lush new growth replaces the rootplate.

Far right above: the largest tree in the garden Monterey Cypress now fallen.

Far right below: Regeneration of New Zealand Christmas Trees, **Metrosideros excelsa**.

101

*Left: Abbey Hill to
St Mary's two
years after the
hurricane with
much work still to
be done.
(Frank Gibson)*

Right: **Protea**
cynaroides.

THE PLANTS

Right:The Middle Terrace: **Aeonium atropurpureum** *and* **Cordyline indivisa**. *(Andrew Lawson)*

THE PLANTS

New Year's Day Flowering List

Certain gardens in Europe have the capacity to grow a wide range of flowering plants that will produce flower in the winter months. It has also been tradition in one or two of these gardens to catalogue a New Year's Day List. The Hanbury Garden at La Mortola on the French/Italian border, a garden very similar to Tresco has on many occasions compiled such a list.

If Tresco had to be twinned with any garden it would be the Hanbury. Growing on the edge of the sea protected from the north by hillsides and usually free from frost and unpleasant climatic temperatures, both gardens have the capacity to cultivate a huge range of plants from the Mediterranean regions of the world. In 1883 a list of the species in flower was recorded in the first week in January in the Hanbury Garden. This was resurrected at The Hanbury by well-known plantsman Roy Lancaster and botanist Michael Lear in the late 1980s. Inspired by this, Tresco has attempted to do the same. It is worth recording that the first such list was made by Augustus Smith.

Our New Year's Day list is quite unique among the gardens of Britain, due to the wide ranging collection held within the gardens and shelterbelts. Across Britain you may find many gardens that hold plants of a similar nature but very few if any have our extensive collection growing outdoors. Our ability to grow plants from the Mediterranean and the dry regions of the world shows up very strongly: a wide range of families is represented and ideally the garden needs to be visited throughout the year to appreciate the full extent of the plant collection.

This list illustrates very clearly the special nature of Tresco Abbey Garden. The diversity of growing and flourishing flowering plants in what for Britain would be a quiet period shows how extraordinary the collection is.

Proteaceae is well represented with Leucadendron, Banksia, Grevillea, Hakea and Protea the dominant groups. Of special note is *Protea eximia*, one of the spoon-bract sugarbush type, also *Protea neriifolia* of the bearded sugar-bush group. Needing a mild climate, movement of air and a soil almost devoid of nutrients the conditions on Tresco are near perfect for protea cultivation. Most spectacular of all the Proteas is *Protea cynaroides*, the king protea. This is an upright or spreading shrub with long stalked leaves and huge flower heads of creamy white flowers surrounded by pointed red or pink bracts up to 30cm (12in) across. It is native of South Africa and enjoys poor sandy soils with good air exposure. Sitting on rocky outcrops it ranks in the top ten of our garden plants that visitors like to see in flower.

Banksia marginata can be seen in flower throughout the year with its yellow bottlebrush-like flowers and can attain a height of over 21m (70ft). A native of New South Wales, Victoria and South Australia it is easily grown and very tolerant of the sea breezes and gales it encounters. *Banksia littoralis*, the swamp banksia, grows extremely well in sandy conditions but will take some years to reach flowering being rather slow growing, but its latin name *littoralis* (of the seashore) means it is very well suited to Tresco. *Banksia integrifolia* is by far the largest of the group, growing into a robust tree of up to 18m (60ft). Its yellow cylindrical flower can be seen at all times of the year and the plants withstand the most ferocious of winter gales and drought-ridden summers with equal measure to no ill effect.

Leucadendron species from South Africa are characterised by the production of showy, coloured leaf bracts often mistaken for flowers, which although attractive are often insignificant. *Leucadendron tinctum* is a bushy spreading shrub with red-tinged leaf bracts that are always easy to spot when sitting amongst other shrubs. *Leucadendron argenteum*

Above:
Banksia caleyi.

106

Left: **Protea
susannae**.
(Alasdair Moore)

Below: **Banksia
littoralis**.

the South African silver tree grows on the Cape peninsula and even on Tresco is considered to be something rather special. A large shrub or small tree it has narrow silvery leaves with a small insignificant flower that lies hidden deep amongst its heads of foliage. It is very attractive when young and can stand full exposure to the Atlantic gales. Most of the plants on Tresco sit high on the upper terraces to gain full advantage of the breeze. If planted in a sheltered position it often sulks and dies back due to lack of air movement. Plants of *Leucadendron argenteum* are not long-lived and need constant replacement.

Hakea suaveolens from Australia produces flowers from early November. Small globes of creamy white flowers sit amongst the needle-like leaves. On the top terrace of the garden Hakea grows quickly and easily from seed, making a large shrub or small tree in four to five years. When flowering has finished woody seedpods containing just one or two seeds are produced which cling tenaciously to the

Above:
Protea neriifolia.

Left:
Banksia victoriae.

trees' branches. Still in Australia *Grevillea rosmariniifolia* "Tresco form", a plant that originated on Tresco produces red flower spikes up to 7.6cm (3in) across. *Grevillea* "Canberra Gem" is a yellow flowering cousin that also does well in the winter months.

Tresco houses the Acacia collection for the NCCPG (National Collection for the Conservation of Plants and Gardens). There are over six hundred National Plant Collections involved in saving and protecting species from disappearing completely from cultivation. The aim of the group is to conserve, document, promote and make available, either through exchange or the commercial sector, Britain's great diversity of garden plants. The *Acacia* group has up to twelve hundred species and cultivars mostly from Australia. The Tresco collection is a modest eighty-five. New Year's Day will find a good number of Acacia in flower both in the garden and within the shelterbelts upon the hillsides where much of our collection exists. *Acacia armata* grows freely on the hillside; with bright yellow globular flowers it can withstand both drought and excess wet. It is a tough plant that also tolerates salt wind very well.

The Cootamundra wattle, *Acacia baileyana*, is very fast growing - still with the typical bright yellow globular flowers. One of the most beautiful species has both a purple and golden form. *Acacia verticillata* has all the appearance of a European gorse bush from a distance. On closer inspection it does possess leaves with sharp points and a flower not unlike a yellow 'jelly bean'. *Acacia longifolia* is probably the quickest growing and most prolific in flower and foliage production on an annual basis. Up to 3m (10ft) a year can

Left:
Malaphore crocea var crocea.

Above: **Euryops chrysanthemoides**.

be added to the overall size of these large spreading shrubs. It produces long rods of yet again bright yellow flowers up to 10cm (4in) long. Bushes respond so well to annual pruning that as a means of extra revenue flower from *Acacia longifolia* is cut from January to March for the flower markets of Britain. Abbey gardeners are despatched in early morning forays about the garden to bring in material ready to be boxed in the packing sheds. This has to be then processed and bunched before packing. Anything up to fifty boxes a day are despatched to markets across Britain such as Covent Garden, Southampton, Birmingham, Bristol and Manchester, so something the garden visitor may note down as merely a plant in flower, can have quite a story behind it.

Climbing plants are well subscribed: one noticed immediately is *Bomarea caldasii*, a showy climber, native of Columbia and Ecuador growing in the Andes in forests at altitudes of over 1000m (3300ft) and which on Tresco regularly entangles itself through the statuesque *Quercus ilex* hedges. Another climber *Hardenbergia comptoniana* from Australia, which was originally planted in the garden in 1904, is noticeable by its violet blue flowers. It is of the Leguminosae family and known by the name of Western Australian coral pea; its tendrils are capable of hanging on to the smallest crevice. On the well sheltered middle terrace is *Tecomaria capensis*, or Cape honeysuckle, which grows through the highly scented *Jasminum polyanthemum*

Left:
Cytisus maderensis.

Far Left:
Hakea suaveolens.

from China. The largest and most tender honeysuckle in flower during the winter months is *Lonicera hildebrandiana*, an evergreen with large leathery leaves and long narrow scented flowers up to 20cm (8in). A native of Burma it can survive temperatures to −3C. *Dolichos lignosus* is frequently used in the garden as a quick growing screen; a rampant climber from Australia it has rose, mauve and white pea flowers covering every centimetre of foliage. *Iochroma fuschoides,* although not strictly a climber, can with support and shelter from a wall be planted with good effect, its trumpet-like flowers drooping in clusters through its very attractive leaves.

Many plants from New Zealand will flower from January onwards. *Metrosideros villosus* the not so well known relation of the Rata, *Metrosideros robusta*, produces its flower later in the year. *Meryta sinclairii* belonging to the family Araliaceae is the broadest-leaved of the New Zealand shrubs, so loved by the Maoris that it took on a religious significance for them and places of worship were sited around the plants.

Leptospermum, the Australian tea tree, abounds throughout the garden but does particularly well on the Abbey hillsides amongst the shelterbelts. Growing in thickets almost impossible to penetrate they seed themselves freely and regular pruning expeditions often take place in order to pass through them. *Leptospermum scoparium* grows into a small tree and is native of New South Wales and Tasmania. It produces masses of white, pink or red flowers that contrast well with the small pointed leaves that are silky when young. Numerous cultivars have been produced and are widely grown in Australia, New Zealand and California as popular garden ornamentals.

The Chilean National flower, *Lapageria rosea* with its thick, waxy red pendulous flower does well in the winter months, its woody stems clambering up the trunks and branches of nearby trees.

In the deep recess of the Old Abbey lives a specimen of *Saurauja subspinosa*, its bell-shaped pale pink flowers with a deep red tube within when viewed from beneath. Planted in 1950 it is a relatively new introduction to the garden.

South Africa has probably one of the largest groups flowering in January. As previously mentioned briefly the Proteaceae supply a large number. There are also such gems as *Coleonema album* and *Coleonema pulchrum* with delicate white and pale pink flowers covering the growing tips. Both have highly scented and aromatic foliage.

Dominant in the flower count are the Aloes, particularly *Aloe arborescens* which flowers from Christmas onwards. The plants form large, many branched shrubs of about 2m(6ft) high. The leaves are sickle-shaped and the flowers come in

Top right:
Aloe sp.

Right: **Clethra arborea**.
(Frank Naylor)

scarlet, orange, pink or yellow. In South Africa it is widely used as a garden ornamental and even as a hedge to protect agricultural fields or animal stock. *Aloe plicatalis* belongs to the group of tree Aloes that have stiff flat leaves with a smooth surface. The leaf arrangement is very striking and often a favourite as a houseplant.

Staying with the succulents, *Agave filifera* from the deserts of Mexico sends up flower spikes at any time of the year although predominantly it is summer flowering. The lower spike will grow up to 2.5m (8ft) tall. *Agave ferox* has also been known to begin its staggering flower growth in the winter months. It is nicknamed the century plant due to the flower supposedly arriving after one hundred years. In fact this is not at all the case and when the plant does flower its flower spikes have been known to reach up to 9m (30ft). This period of growth can take up to twelve to fifteen weeks. The energy expended by the plant is such that it then dies. All is not lost however, seed is produced and in many cases there are young plantlets around the base of the parent. These survive to produce the next generation.

Tumbling around them over the rocks are plants of *Lampranthus*, members of a group with over two hundred and twenty seven species. This group of succulent plants

Left:
Yucca gloriosa.

does well on the dry, free-draining cliffs within the garden. Tresco hold a modest collection and most are summer flowering but a small number can be seen occasionally producing flower for the flower count.

Abundant all over the garden is the species of *Pelargonium*, also from South Africa, with many of the "Unique" hybrids in flower. *Pelargonium* "Scarlet Unique" and *Pelargonium* "Moores Victory" are just two that stand out. *Pelargonium tomentosum* has naturalised on Tresco escaping the garden to colonise the hillsides within the shelter of the windbreaks. Although mentioned in the list for flowering purposes it is principally grown for its very soft peppermint scented leaves. The flower sits above the foliage with small pale pink and white petals. It is not unknown for the large hillside drifts to be cut to ground level with a lawn mower doing absolutely no harm to the plant. Pelargoniums on Scilly are perennials and the growing problems are more of containment than winter protection. Growth can be so rampant throughout the year that pruning can take place three or four times.

From the family Compositae come the Osteospermums. *Osteospermum* "Tresco Peggy" was reputedly collected by Commander Tom Dorrien–Smith from Cape Town and named after his wife. Its deep purple flowers produce a colourful display at most times of the year. The plants form expansive mats of vegetation that cascade over small cliffs to show off the flower to best effect.

The tree heaths, *Erica canaliculata*, *Erica lusitanica* and *Erica arborea* begin to show themselves in late November and continue through well into the New Year; by late January they dominate the top terrace of the garden along with their smaller and more decorative cousins *Erica verticillata* and *Erica versicolour*. Both belong to a group where the flowers are borne at the end of the branches and tend to be very showy.

Albizia lophantha from Australia, named after the Italian naturalist, and of the Leguminosae family is in flower throughout the year. Often confused with Acacia due to its foliage, it seeds freely about the garden and the yellow brush-like flowers often form in pairs.

Also flowering around the calendar are the *Correa* species, members of Rutaceae, a family of evergreen shrubs native to Australia and Tasmania. Known for their bell-like flowers, many varieties have been raised under cultivation. The cultivars on Tresco include *Correa reflexa* "Dusky Bell", a spreading shrub up to two metres (7ft) high, it is an old cultivar known for at least fifty years. *Correa pulchella*, a very attractive pink or red flowering shrub from South Australia, it is also tolerant of drought and can be used to good effect as ground cover. As a coastal plant the Correas thrive and *Correa alba* is both tolerant of wind and salt.

Lower, and in the more shaded area of the garden, lurks *Luculia pinceana* from Assam: an evergreen shrub with rounded heads of scented pale pink flowers, which are very welcome in the early part of the year.

Still in the lower garden, a plant not normally grown for its flower but rather for its foliage, is *Astelia* "Silver Spear". A herbaceous perennial from New Zealand, its creamy yellow flower is to be found among the shining tufts of foliage. It is a very handsome plant with distinctive silvery

Left:
Metrosideros excelsa.

NEW YEAR'S DAY FLOWERING

1: *Arctotis aspers.*

2: *Acacia verticillata.*

3: *Cytisus fragrans*

4: *Aloe arborescens.*

sword-like leaves: it is a native of the Chatham Islands and enjoys a moist soil and cool position. It is not always easy to find on Tresco.

Brugmansia sanguinea, or to use its former name which may be more familiar, *Datura sanguinea*, is a native of South America. Growing at altitudes of up to 1000m (3300ft), plants can reach a growing height on Tresco of up to 6m (20ft). Its vivid orange and yellow trumpets up to 25cm (10in) long hang down through the canopy of velvety foliage. They are frequently grown in their native country for medicinal and narcotic properties.

Bulbous plants play a strong part within the Abbey Garden and probably the showiest of all is *Amaryllis belladonna*, the "Jersey Lily", from South Africa. Succulent pink scented flowers sit on a long, bare, leafed stem. The foliage from the bulb dies back in the summer months to expose the bulb to the summer sun. In the autumn when the bulb has ripened, the flowers appear in great profusion. It is grown to great effect along path and wall edges within the garden, using the reflected heat to enhance flowering.

From the Eastern Cape in South Africa comes *Nerine bowdenii*, which produces funnel-shaped gently scented pink flowers. Normally grown under glass it flowers best when the bulbs are congested.

Growing in the shade of the Abbey Hill on the drive sits *Sparmannia africana*, native of South Africa in the southern part of Cape Province. A shrub with very large leaves of up to 25cm (10in) across, it is covered in small white flowers with numerous stamens that when touched expand as if awakening from sleep. Growing up to 6m (20ft) tall its lime green leaf makes it stand out from the crowd. Rising even higher skyward tower groves of *Clethra arborea* from Madeira. This tree has shiny evergreen leaves and spikes of scented white cup-shaped flowers. Growing on Tresco up to 20m (70ft) tall, it enjoys a peaty soil and will seed freely if left to its own devices.

Hymonosporum flavum is an upright evergreen from Queensland and a member of the *Pittosporum* family. Growing in rainforests it has adapted well to the shady and warm Long Walk in the centre of the garden. The tubular creamy flowers turn yellow and orange as they age, giving the effect of a multi-coloured tree.

Many of the plants included within the flower count have been native in the garden for many years. In this way a high proportion have seeded themselves naturally. To plant lovers they may give the impression of being planted in just the right spot when in reality the gardeners' weeding programme has created this effect. Plants that come into this category are many and varied.

Acacia melanoxylon, the Blackwood Acacia from Australia, is a large upright tree with large globular flower heads in pale yellow. Once the tree has grown it can become a nuisance by producing copious suckers, giving the false appearance of a grove of specimens. On Tresco it grows very well on the shelterbelt hillsides where it has the space to grow to its maximum height of 30m (100ft).

Coronilla valentina is easily spotted in the garden during the winter months. Bright golden yellow flowers shine out from above the foliage in dull weather. An evergreen shrub from the Mediterranean, it performs well all year.

Fascicularia pitcairniifolia in the family Bromeliaceae is from Chile in South America. It produces a double impact with both flower and inner rosette leaves bearing colour. It is a stemless epiphytic perennial that produces huge ground-covering clumps which march across the ground in all directions. With leaves up to 1m (3ft) long, edged with short brown spreading spines, the flower hides away set back into the head of brightly coloured red foliage, giving the appearance of a small explosion. When in need of pruning often the best choice of tool is a chainsaw as the plant grows with such vigour.

Geranium maderense is normally a spring/summer flowering plant from Madeira which, from time to time, flowers out of season. From seed it will need up to three years growth before producing a flower. Over many years it has held a position close to the top of the all time garden favourites for visitors to Tresco. A huge rosette of flowers sits above its own foliage in a pink and purple eruption. Without doubt it is the most spectacular of all the Geranium species.

Agapanthus praecox orientalis from the southern and eastern Cape is completely rampant not just in the garden confines but living amongst sand dunes, on walls and buildings: many hundreds of thousands now inhabit Tresco. An evergreen perennial, the plant will form vast clumps before sending up dense heads of blue flowers. Even though doing well enough on sand, if fed, in good ground, the plant will thrive to a higher level.

Plants in Flower on New Year's Day

Abutilon vitifolium	Chile
Acacia armata	Australia
Acacia baileyana	Australia
Acacia dealbata	Australia
Acacia falciformis	Australia
Acacia longifolia	Australia
Acacia melonoxylon	Australia
Acacia mucronata	Australia
Acacia retinoides	Australia
Acacia saligna	Australia
Acacia O shaunesii	Australia
Acacia podalyriifolia	Australia
Acacia verticillata	Australia
Aeonium domesticum	Canary Islands
Agapanthus orientalis	South Africa
Agave filifera	Mexico
Agonis marginata	Australia
Albizia lophanthera	Australia
Aloe arborescens	Cape Province
Aloe dawei	Uganda
Aloe plicatilis	Cape Province
Aloe saponaria	Cape Province
Aloe shelpii	Ethiopia
Aloe succotrina	Cape Province
Amaryllis belladonna	South Africa
Anigozanthus flavidus	Australia
Arctotis aspera	South Africa
Argyranthemum frutescens	Canary Islands
Aristea thyrsiflorus	South Africa
Arthropodium cirrhatum	New Zealand
Astelia grandis	New Zealand
Banksia caleyi	Australia
Banksia ericifolia	Australia
Banksia integrifolia	Australia
Banksia littoralis	Australia
Banksia marginata	Australia
Banksia ornata	Australia
Banksia praemorsa	Australia
Banksia victoriae	Australia
Berberis darwinii	Chile
Bergenia cordifolia	Siberia
Bomarea caldesii	Ecuador
Buddleia salvifolia	South Africa
Calothamnus pinifolius	Australia
Camellia "Adolphe Audusson"	Hort
Camellia japonica "Montironi"	Hort
Camellia japonica "Althiiflora"	Hort

Camellia japonica "Anna Grumeau"	Hort
Camellia japonica "Snow Princess"	Hort
Camellia japonica var Magnoliiflora	Hort
Camellia japonica "Rogetsii"	Hort
Camellia japonica "Lady Clare"	Hort
Camellia williamsii "J.C.Williams"	Hort
Camellia williamsii "Mary Jobson"	Hort
Camellia williamsii "Rosemary Williams"	Hort
Camellia williamsii "St Ewe"	Hort
Canarina canariensis	Canary Islands
Canna iridiflora	Peru
Carpobrotus edulis	South Africa
Cestrum fasciculatun "Newellii"	Hort
Cestrum parqui	Chile
Chlorophytum comosum "Variegatum"	South Africa
Choisya ternata	Mexico
Chrysocoma aurea	South Africa
Cistus x corbariensis	Mediterranean
Clethra arborea	Madeira
Cobaea scandens	Mexico
Coleonema album	South Africa
Coleonema pulchrum	South Africa
Colletia cruciata	Uruguay
Convolvulous sabiatus	North Africa
Coprosma robusta	New Zealand
Corokia parviflora	New Zealand
Coronilla glauca	Southern Europe
Correa "Dusky Bell"	Australia
Correa alba	Australia
Correa backhousiana	Australia
Correa decumbens	Australia

Left:
Kunzea baxteri.

Cytisus maderensis	Madeira	*Hebe speciosa*	New Zealand
Datura aurea	Columbia	*Hebe speciosa var violaceae*	New Zealand
Datura sanguinea	Peru	*Helichrysum felinum*	South Africa
Delosperma aberdensis	South Africa	*Helleborus corsicus*	Sardinia
Delosperma lehmannii	South Africa	*Hydrangea macrophylla hybrids*	China
Dolichos globosus	Australia	*Hymenosporum flavum*	Australia
Drimys winteri	South America	*Hypericum canariense*	Canary Islands
Echium x scilloniensis	Hort	*Isoplexus sceptrum*	Canary Islands
Elegia capensis	South Africa	*Jasminum polyanthemum*	China
Entelia arborescens	New Zealand	*Kennedia nigricans*	Australia
Erica canaliculata	South Africa	*Kunzea ambigua*	Australia
Erica cerinthiodes	South Africa	*Kunzea baxteri*	Australia
Erica cruenta	South Africa	*Lampranthus aurantiacus*	South Africa
Erica diaphana	South Africa	*Lampranthus blandus*	South Africa
Erica discolor	South Africa	*Lampranthus formosus*	South Africa
Erica dolliformis	South Africa	*Lampranthus zeyheri*	South Africa
Erica glandulosa	South Africa	*Lapageria rosea*	Chile
Erica hebecalyx	South Africa	*Lavendula spica*	Mediterranean
Erica lateralis	South Africa	*Leonotis leonurus*	South Africa
Erica versicolor	South Africa	*Leptospermum* "Coral Candy"	Australasia
Erica viridescens	South Africa	*Leptospermum grandiflorum*	Tasmania
Erigeron mucronatus	Mexico	*Leptospermum lanigerum*	Australia
Eriocephalus sericeus	South Africa	*Leptospermum scoparium*	New Zealand
Escallonia macrantha "Apple Blossom"	Hort	*Leucadendron tinctum*	South Africa
Escallonia rubra "Macrantha"	Chile	*Libertia peregrinans*	New Zealand
Eucalyptus pulverulenta	Australia	*Litsea japonica*	Japan
Eupatorium micranthum	Mexico	*Lobelia laxiflora*	Mexico
Euryops athanasiae	South Africa	*Luculia gratissima*	Himalaya
Euryops chrysanthemoides	South Africa	*Mahonia aquifolium*	North America
Fascicularia pitcairnifolia	South America	*Mahonia pinnata*	California
Fatsia japonica	Japan	*Medicago arborea*	Southern Europe
Felicia amelloides	South Africa	*Melaleuca radula*	Australia
Fuchsia arborescens	Chile	*Melaleuca hypericifolia*	Australia
Fuchsia boliviana	South America	*Meryta sinclairii*	New Zealand
Fuchsia "Lady Boothby"	Hort	*Metrosideros kermadecencis* "Variegata"	New Zealand
Fuchscia megallanica	Chile	*Metrosideros excelsa*	New Zealand
Fuchsia microphylla	Chile	*Metrosideros villosa*	New Zealand
Gazania splendens	South Africa	*Mitraria coccinea*	Chile
Geranium maderense	Madeira	*Musschia woolastonii*	Madeira
Grevillea "Canberra Gem"	Australia	*Narcissus* "Newton"	Hort
Grevillea "Olympic Flame"	Australia	*Narcissus* "Peshawar"	Hort
Grevillea lanigera	Australia	*Narcissus* "Scilly White"	Hort
Grevillea rosmarinifolia	Australia	*Narcissus* "Soleil d'Or"	Hort
Grevillea x semperflorens	Australia	*Narcissus* "Paper White"	Hort
Hakea suaveolens	Australia	*Neopanax laetum*	New Zealand
Halleria lucida	South Africa	*Nerine bowdenii*	South Africa
Hebe x andersonii	Hort	*Nerium oleander*	Southern Europe
Hebe x lewisii	Hort	*Ochagavia carnea*	Chile
Hebe odora	New Zealand	*Oscularia deltoides*	South Africa

Osteospermum ecklonis	South Africa
Osteospermum jacundum	South Africa
Osteospermum "Tresco Peggy"	South Africa
Oxalis pes-caprae	Bermuda
Ozothamnus "Sussex Silver"	Australia
Passiflora caerulea	Peru
Pelargonium "Atomic Snowflake"	Hort
Pelargonium "Attar of Roses"	Hort
Pelargonium "Endsleigh"	Hort
Pelargonium "Lady Plymouth"	Hort
Pelargonium "Moores Victory"	Hort
Pelargonium "Pink Capitatum"	Hort
Pelargonium "Rollissons Unique"	Hort
Pelargonium "Scarlet Unique"	Hort
Pelargonium "Stella"	Hort
Pelargonium "The Boar"	Hort
Pelargonium x Blandfordianum	Hort
Pelargonium crispum	South Africa
Pelargonium cucullatum	South Africa
Pelargonium fragrans	Hort
Pelargonium glutinosum	South Africa
Pelargonium papilionaceum	South Africa
Pelagonium peltatum	South Africa
Pelargonium radens	South Africa
Pelargonium tomentosum	South Africa
Petasites fragrans	Southern Europe
Pittosporum bicolor	Australia
Pittosporum crassifolium	New Zealand
Pittosporum tobira	Japan
Polygala myrtifolia	South Africa
Pomaderris elliptica	Australia
Protea aurea	South Africa
Protea compacta	South Africa
Protea cynaroides	South Africa
Protea eximia	South Africa
Protea lepidocarpodendron	South Africa
Protea mundii	South Africa
Protea neriifolia	South Africa
Protea obtusifolia	South Africa
Protea susannae	South Africa
Rosmarinus officinalis	Mediterranean
Ruscus aculeatus	Mediterranean
Salvia fulgens	Mexico
Salvia grahamii	Mexico
Salvia involucrata	Mexico
Salvia leucantha	Mexico
Senecio petasites	Mexico
Solanun laciniatum	Australia
Sollya heterophylla	Australia

Sonchus congestus	Canary Islands
Sparmannia africana	South Africa
Sphaeralcea umbellata	Mexico
Strobilanthes dyerianus	Burma
Tecomaria capensis	South Africa
Telanthophora grandifolia	Mexico
Tetrapanax papyifera	China
Tibouchina semidecandra	Brazil
Trymalium ledifolium	Australia
Ulex europaeus	Western Europe
Viburnum farreri	China
Viburnum tinus	Southern Europe
Vinca major	North East Asia
Viola odorata	Southern Europe
Virgilea oroboides	South Africa
Watsonia galpinii	South Africa
Westringia eremicola	Australia
Yucca gloriosa	South West U.S.A

Left: **Banksia praemorsa** "Red Form".

Right: The Succulent Rockery above the Old Abbey.

Spring and Summer Flowering List

Abutilon vitifolium	Chile
Acacia armata	Australia
Acacia longifolia	Australia
Acacia riceana	Australia
Acacia verticillata	Australia
Aeonium arboreum "Atropurpureum"	Canary Isles
Aeonium sp	Canary Isles
Agapanthus orientalis	South Africa
Aloe arborescens	South Africa
Aloe striatula	South Africa
Arctotis aspera	South Africa
Banksia cayleyi	Australia
Banksia grandis	Australia
Banksia integrifolia	Australia
Banksia praemorsa "Red Form"	Australia
Bomarea caldesii	Ecuador
Boronia alata	Australia
Carpobrotus edulis	South Africa
Ceanothus arboreus	California
Chasmanthe bicolor	South Africa
Chrysanthemum frutescens	Canary Isles
Chrysocoma aurea	South Africa
Clianthus puniceus	New Zealand
Coleonema album	South Africa
Cordyline australis	New Zealand
Corokia buddleoides	New Zealand
Coronilla gluaca	Southern Europe
Correa virens	Australia
Crinum bulbispermum	Natal
Cytisus maderensis	Madeira
Datura sanguinea	Peru
Dianella tasmanica	Tasmania
Doryanthes palmeri	Australia
Drimys winteri	South America
Drosanthemum floribundum	South Africa
Dryandra formosa	Australia
Echium pininiana	Canary Isles
Echium x scilloniensis	
Echium webbii	Canary Isles
Entelea arborescens	New Zealand
Erica arborea	Southern Europe
Erica canaliculata	South Africa
Erica versicolor	South Africa
Euryops pectinatus	South Africa
Euphorbia mellifera	Canary Isles
Fuchsia magellanica	Chile
Gazania splendens	South Africa

Right:
Leucadendron sp.

Left: **Veltheimia
bracteata.**

Spring and Summer Flowering

1: *Cordyline australis.*

2: *Scilla peruviana.*

3: *Banksia grandis.*

4: *Leucadendron sp.*

5: *Acacia riceana.*

6: *Dryandra formosa.*

Geranium canariense	Canary Isles
Geranium maderense	Madeira
Geranium palmatum	Canary Isles
Greyii sutherlandii	Natal
Griselinia lucida	New Zealand
Gunnera manicata	Chile
Helichrysum felinum	South Africa
Homaria collina	South Africa
Isoplexus canariensis	Canary Isles
Ixia spp	South Africa
Kennedya rubicunda	Australia
Kunzea baxteri	Australia
Lampranthus sp	South Africa
Leptospermum scoparium	New Zealand
Leucadendron discolor	South Africa
Leucadendron sp	South Africa
Lonicera hilderbrandiana	Soth East Asia
Metrosideros excelsa	New Zealand
Metrosideros robusta	New Zealand
Neopanax laetum	New Zealand
Olearia angustifolia	New Zealand
Olearia X scilloniensis	
Osteospermum ecklonis	South Africa
Osteospermum "Tresco Peggy"	South Africa
Ozothamnus rosmarinifolius	Australia
Pelargonium cucullatum	South Africa
Pelargonium papilionaceum	South Africa
Pittosporum crassifolium	Chatham Islands
Phlomis fruticosa	Greece
Protea eximia	South Africa
Protea lepidocarpodendron	South Africa
Psoralea affinis	South Africa
Puya chilensis	Chile
Rosmarinus officinalis	Mediterranean
Scilla peruviana	Portugal
Senecio glastifolius	South Africa
Senecio petasites	Mexico
Sophora tetraptera	New Zealand
Sparmannia africana	South Africa
Veltheima bracteata	South Africa
Wisteria floribunda	Japan

Right:
Echium webbii.

Left: **Lonicera hilderbrandiana.**

Right: **Geranium maderense**.
(Frank Naylor)

130

Correa species.
(Frank Naylor)

The following brief descriptions and plant selection are to give an indication of the plants that as a growing collection form the spirit behind the Abbey Garden. I hope it shows the special range that is so unique to Tresco.

From the rainforests of New Zealand, the cliffs of Madeira, to the Cape of South Africa and the coasts of California the extra-ordinary growing conditions experienced by our plants in such a small area are to be found nowhere else in Britain, if not the world.

It would have been very easy to make the list longer with 'special' plants but I hope you will get a feel for the garden from my choice.

Abutilon vitifolium

Aeonium cuneatum

Aeonium tabulaeforme

A. arboreum atropurpureum

Abutilon

A fast growing shrub/tree which is a native of Southern Chile. It grows very easily from seed and establishes quickly, growing up to 7.5m (25ft) in height. Large flowers sometimes up to 7.6 - 10cm (3-4in) across. It belies its tender appearance by its toleration of salt gales, drought conditions and cold temperatures. One species we grow well on Tresco is *A. vitifolium* with white or pale blue flowers, which is in many shrub borders throughout the garden.

Acacia

Over eighty species and cultivars are held in the garden. Many will flower from November through to the late summer months. Flowers will range in colour from pale yellow to bright. A vast range of habit and size from shrubs such as *A. lineata* a spreading plant to tall trees such as *A. decurrens* which will grow up to 15m (50ft). Tresco holds a collection for the National Council for Conservation of Plants and Gardens. *Acacia longifolia,*

Acacia longifolia

Acacia species

Acacia verticillata and *Acacia melanoxylon* readily seed themselves on the hill-sides around the garden.

Aeonium

One plant that typifies the style of gardening on Tresco. Many species self sow themselves not just within the garden but across the island. *A. cuneatum* is a succulent perennial that is stemless and produces a flower of golden yellow up to 1m (3ft). Predominately from the Canary Isles. *Aeonium arboreum* "Zwartkop" is always popular with visitors with a distinct purple colouration.

Aloe striatula

Agapanthus inapertus

Aloe mitriformis

Agapanthus

Tresco is probably the most suitable place in Britain to grow Agapanthus out of doors. Hot dry summers and warm winters provide perfect conditions for these evergreen perennials from South Africa. *A. preacox subspecies orientalis* seeds itself freely not just in the garden but many hundreds of thousands grow in the surrounding sand dunes. Long stemmed heads of blue and white flowers are produced in July and August. As a cut flower it is very long lasting.

Agave

A group of perennial succulents from the deserts of Mexico and North America. This genus is noted for the sharp terminal spines and toothed leaf edges. Never a popular plant when weeding nearby, nicknamed "The Century Plant" due to the supposed flowering of the plant after one hundred years. In fact many of the plants are monocarpic: only flowering once in their lives. Agaves are important dot or feature plants and will always produce a bold effect.

Agave americana

Agave ferox

Aloe

As a winter flowering plant on Tresco the genus *Aloe* is hard to beat. A succulent, growing in a range of habits from plants with stems and trunks to rambling, creeping, speckled, spotted and dwarf types. Most of the species we have are South African. They have an architectural quality even when not in flower. *Aloe arborescens* is a species that is abundant on Tresco and grows very well on our granite soil with its large scarlet flowers showing above the foliage from late November to February. Although generally frost tender one or two species such as *A. striatula* can tolerate extremely low temperatures and can go on to make large attractive bushes.

Amaryllis belladonna (pink)

Amaryllis belladonna (white)

Amaryllis

In the late summer months very few plants can compete with the large pink exuberant trumpets of *A. belladonna*. The lush green foliage dies back in the early summer feeding the bulb before its flower push. Planted around our path edges it is very effective in lines or as single groups.

Araucaria heterophylla

Araucaria

The Norfolk Island Pine or *A. heterophylla* is one of a group of conifers containing eighteen species. Introduced to Tresco in 1851 it has a distinct foliage that sets it apart from many other trees with a series of branches evenly spaced and regular. Grown in groups or avenues they are very striking and have in the past before storm damage grown to a height of at least 27m (90ft).

Arctotis

At any one time of the year flower may be found on the plant *Arctotis aspera* with its daisy-like flower of up to 7.6cm (3in) in diameter. A plant capable of living on both cliff face and herbaceous border it has great flexibility. It may be cut back very hard to ground level to improve vigour and will withstand both drought and cold temperature, reshooting from root systems if it has need. Many annual members are used about the garden to increase colour in the summer months giving an impression of the South African Veldt flora.

Astelia

Enjoying damp and shady garden positions, these handsome foliage plants from the forests of New Zealand form large clumps of arching, linear leaves covered in silvery white scales. *A. chathamica* and *A. nervosa* are the better known species. They produce a flower spike of green or yellow followed by orange or red berries.

Banksia integrifolia (Frank Naylor)

Banksia praemorsa (Frank Naylor)

Banksia coccinea (Frank Naylor)

Beschorneria yuccoides (Frank Naylor)

Banksia

One of the more important plant groups within the Abbey Garden. This Australian genus is represented by over thirty-five species in our own collection. Contained in the family Proteaceae these plants thrive on soil low in phosphates and nitrates – perfect for Tresco. Cultivated for both flower and foliage they are evergreen and will tolerate a small amount of frost. Very good in drought and exposed coastal conditions they add a real flavour of the Australian outback to the garden. *Banksia integrifolia* will grow up to 18m (60ft) high and always has a bottlebrush yellow flower in evidence. *Banksia grandis* can produce flowers up to 33.5cm (14in) long perched above its own foliage.

Beschorneria

These clump forming perennials from Mexico with sword-like leaves produce a flower spike well in excess of 2m (6ft) long. The green flowers protrude from red bracts in the late spring/early summer. Grown in full sun they form self-perpetuating colonies over a period of years.

Bomarea

Tresco does not easily grow plants from the more tropical regions of South America but one plant that always stands out especially when in flower is the climber from Ecuador, *Bomarea caldasii*. Only the one species is grown on Tresco even though the genus contains around one hundred and twenty members of the group. Narrow funnel shaped flowers up to 5cm (2in) long, red/orange on the outside and orange/yellow on the inside. Flowering in summer months they can be seen scrambling through the evergreen oak hedges that protect Tresco from the winter gales.

Brachyglottis

A genus that has been split to include many of the group known as *Senecio* in a past life. *B. greyii* from New Zealand forms an open mound covered in bright yellow flowerheads. One particular plant stands out not for its flower, but for the magnificent foliage that is produced is *Brachyglottis repanda*. Leaves up to 25cm (10in) long and 20cm (8in) wide are dark green with a white felted underneath. Described by some as the "Postcard Tree" due to this phenomenon.

Brugmansia sanguinea

Brugmansia

From the potato family, Solanaceae comes *Brugmansia suaveolens* from Southeast Brazil. Commonly known as angels trumpets due to the long tubular orange and red flowers. Plants can grow to well over 9m (30ft) high and will regenerate from ground level if cut back by frost.

Callistemon

The Australian Bottlebrush surprisingly has only around twenty-five species. Grown for the colourful terminal flowers which may be red, pink, yellow or green. They can range from fully hardy to frost-tender. *Callistemon citrinus splendens* is popular as a garden plant growing up to 6m (20ft) high. As a wall plant they flourish and can take full sun.

Bomarea caldasii

Callistemon species (Andrew Lawson)

Carpobrotus

One of the most prolific and robust succulents to grow on Tresco. The name is derived from the Greek meaning karpos (fruit) and brota (edible). The common name of Hottontot fig is well chosen and large carpets inhabit south facing banks taking in the sun. They have exceptionally large flowers in purple, pink, white and yellow. Plants are easily grown from cuttings and can tolerate a wide range of soil types. Particularly adept on sand. Many species come from South Africa but also Australia, Tasmania, Chile and California. Flowers will open in the morning and close at night.

Ceanothus

Not many plant species give a blue/ purple flower colour to the garden but *Ceanothus* is one of them. Around fifty species and many cultivars make up a wide range of plant types from small, low, creeping shrubs to small trees. Spring and early summer flowering. Mostly evergreen they are often susceptible to root breakage caused by strong wind. *C. arboreus* "Trewithen Blue" is very popular as a garden plant.

Clianthus puniceus (Frank Naylor)

Chrysanthemum frutescens

Chrysanthemum

Fast growing and quick to make an impression. *Chrysanthemum frutescens*, from the Canary Isles is a good choice to make for anyone wishing for a feel of the Mediterranean. There are several shades of colour and the genus is daisy-flowered and can be annual or perennial. Flowers are produced throughout the year and bushes respond very well to light pruning on a regular basis.

Cistus

A trouble free plant that always performs, the rock rose grows very well on hot, dry, well drained soil. Grown for flower, with showy saucer-like petals of pink, white and purple. Each bloom lasts for only one day but the plant flowers for many weeks. Very easy to raise from seed. *Cistus ladanifer* from the Southwest Mediterranean can grow up to 1.8m (6ft) tall making it attractive at the back of a border.

Clianthus

A genus of only two species, here on Tresco we grow *Clianthus puniceus* or "Lobster Claw" from the North Island of New Zealand. Primarily a wall plant, large clusters of brilliant red flowers hang down through the spring and summer attracting the attention of passing visitors. Cultivars such as the white flowered *Clianthus puniceus albus* and *Clianthus puniceus* "Flamingo" with dark rose flowers give a variation. Plants do respond well to being cut back after three or four years to introduce vigour. Will need to grow in full sun for maximum effect.

Coleonema

One of the most delightful South African shrubs in the garden. Highly scented foliage is typical of the Rutaceae family. We grow two of the eight species on Tresco. Enjoying hot and dry conditions both *Coleonema album*, with white flower and *Coleonema pulchrum* with pink flower excel themselves from spring onwards. The plant is always neat, keeps its shape and requires very little work from any passing gardener.

Convolvulus

Related to the Bindweed but nowhere near as troublesome, *Convolvulus mauritanicus* climbs and scrambles it way through other plants' foliage in a very attractive manner. It is a trailing plant, evergreen and produces large numbers of funnel-shaped pale blue flowers. Very slow growing to begin with, once established, plants will last many years. Particularly good in pots with other plants around it.

Coprosma

A plant grown for its shiny foliage and its quality to live in shady areas and tolerate salt spray and wind. Especially good in coastal areas it can be grown as a hedge or as an individual specimen. From New Zealand the genus contains over ninety species. *Coprosma repens*, "The Looking Glass" plant so called because of the glossy leaf will grow up to 9m (30ft) tall. Many varieties have variegated foliage. Ours have withstood periods of frost and snow being cut to ground level, but always reshoot well from the roots.

Cordyline

The New Zealand Cabbage Palm instantly attracts the garden visitor and giving the impression of the tropics. Very fast growth once planted and very easy to grow from seed. Flowering on

Correa species (Frank Naylor)

Tresco in late May to late June, the flowers are highly scented with large heads of white and creamy flowers. In good soil they will develop deep roots in their search for water. If due to cold they lose leaves then most species can be cut back to the branch or trunk to reshoot. We grow *Cordyline australis* both in the garden confines and about the island, as it does well in coastal exposure. *Cordyline indivisa* has a much broader leaf and fewer branches. *Cordyline* "Albertii" a cultivar has attractive cream edges with a red mid-rib.

Cordyline australis (Frank Naylor)

Correa

Often with the genus *Correa* it is not until you are close to the bush that the small tubular fuchsia-like flower is noticed. Very attractive small bushes in a wide range of flower colour, they are in the Rutaceae family and come from Australia. They prefer better soil than they perhaps receive on Tresco and we use one species as a hedge plant again due to its tolerance of salt spray gales: *Correa backhouseana*. A particular favourite is *Correa* "Dusky Bell", flowering in the summer with carmine/red tubular flowers.

Crassula coccinea (Fiona Wilding)

years. *Cupressus macrocarpa* from Monterey, California is very quick growing reaching heights of over 30m (100ft). Easy to grow from seed it often self sows itself and transplants easily. It can be used as a hedge if cut regularly when young. Within the garden the *C. sempervirens* "Pencil Cypress" enhances the feeling of the Mediterranean with its slender outline.

Cyathea

Tresco has always grown many plants from New Zealand even though our dry soils, high sun hours and salt gales do not always suit the larger leaves of many of New Zealand's flora. If how ever a microclimate can be manufactured then the *Cyathea* genus makes a big impact on the garden. In the wild some Cyathea can reach up to 18m (60ft) with fibrous trunks topped by the leaf-bearing rhizome with leaves up to 4.5m (15ft) across. Grown as single specimens or groups for display they are equally effective. The black tree fern, *Cyathea medullaris* is an absolute showstopper.

Crassula

A group of drought tolerant succulents that number up to one hundred and fifty species mostly from South Africa but also Madagascar and Asia. Mainly grown for the leaves they provide a contrast to the other succulent plants in the garden such as the Aloe, Lampranthus and Aeonium. One particular species that we grow for flower is *Crassula coccinea* (formerly *Rochea coccinea*), growing to a height of only 43cm (15in) it has densely packed leaves with bright red tubular flowers that sit above the foliage.

Cupressus

The single most important Genus in the history of the Abbey Garden would probably be *Cupressus*. As the mainstay in the windbreaks they have shielded the garden from the Atlantic gales for over one hundred and sixty

Cyathea medullaris (Frank Naylor)

Doryanthes palmeri

Dryandra

Proteaceae form a large part of the flora on the Top Terrace of the garden and within the genus falls *Dryandra formosa*. It needs to be grown in well drained soil with low fertility (as with Protea). Small 10cm (4in) rounded flowers in bright yellow spheres are produced from early spring right through the summer months. It is often possible to find flower also during winter.

Dryandra formosa (Frank Naylor)

Dasylirion

As an architectural specimen the all year round performance of *Dasylirion* is hard to beat. With leaves over 1m (3ft) long growing into a dense globe of foliage this Yucca-like plant can be used to great effect in garden design. After many years they can form trunks which have no means of support and will sprawl about the ground like a python searching for its lunch. Described as frost tender, on Tresco they have survived temperatures as low as -8C.

Doryanthes

A genus of only two species from Australia. Classed as perennial succulents both species can produce leaves up to 3m (10ft) long. *Doryanthes palmeri* will put up a flower spike 3m (10ft) to 4.5m (15ft) tall, covered with rich red flowers 5cm (2in) across gathered on the stem. Will withstand frost but likes shade to produce its best foliage.

Echium X scilloniensis

Erica canaliculata

Erica versicolor

Echium wildpretii

Erica diaphana

Echium

In the top ten of Tresco at its best will be the *Echium*. From the Canary Islands both the biannual and perennial do well in the garden. *Echium pininana* will grow and flower in a period of just fifteen months, sometimes reaching a height of up to 6m (20ft) and covered in tiny blue flowers. In the first season the stem will grow to 1.8 - 2.5m (6 - 8ft) with long wide leaves. The stem of the plant is covered in tiny hairs, which are painful if touched. *Echium candicans* has the same spike-like flowers on a smaller scale with the flower spike up to 38cm (15in). Plants will only last four to five years at most before becoming broken and untidy. Due to the fragile root system it is almost impossible to transplant unless seedlings. Plants will readily hybridise between the biannual and shrub. *Echium wildpretii* is the smaller red/pink species with a lighter foliage colour.

Erica

Europe can contribute only twenty-one species of heath flora, where South Africa can call on over four hundred. It is to these Cape Heaths that Tresco looks. The vast array of colours and forms are overwhelming. We grow a modest thirty-five. They are broken down into forty-one groups for botanical purpose. Usually quite small they are quite easy to grow from seed especially using the smoke system to assist germination. Not always very long lasting and sometimes will appear to die for almost no reason.

Eucalyptus globulus (Frank Naylor)

Eucalyptus ficifolia

Eucalyptus

Forever associated with Australia, most gardens in Britain would find it possible to grow at least one species of *Eucalyptus* (probably *E. gunnii*). Here our collection numbers well over a hundred species growing outdoors, with many flowering strongly. Among the more spectacular are huge specimens of *E. globulus*, The Tasmanian Blue Gum, so named as new foliage each year, surprisingly, is blue and *Eucalyptus ficifolia* a red and sometimes pink flowering gum that will flower in the late summer/early autumn. Often the best time to view trees is in pouring rain, which brings out the colours of the trunks and bark variation.

Fascicularia

Bromeliads are usually associated with the tropics but on Tresco we grow two species from Chile. Both relatively hardy they can form vast mounds of foliage. *Fascicularia bicolor* and *Fascicularia pitcairniifolia* both with long,

slender and spiny leaves. The leaves turn bright crimson around the flower that nestles in the centre of the inflorescence. Flowers are pale blue or violet.

Furcraea

Sitting like giant "Triffids" the furcraea from Mexico appears to come from another planet. A yucca-like plant that can grow for many years before flowering. In the family Agavaceae it is also monocarpic and will die once it has flowered. The flower spike can produce a 6m (20ft) tall spike in just for to five weeks which then opens out with hundreds of yellow/pale green flowers. Small bulbs are formed on the branchlets of the flower spike and can be planted out.

Furcraea longeava (Frank Naylor)

Fascicularia pitcairniifolia

Gazania species (Andrew Lawson)

Geranium maderense (Frank Naylor)

Gazania

Very popular in many gardens Gazania thrive on hot sunny conditions. From the low altitude plains to the alpine meadows of South Africa they can be annual or perennial. Grown as summer bedding they are long lasting with high colour in the front of the border. *Gazania splendens* will grow for many years keeping its low compact shape and bearing orange or yellow daisy-like flowers.

Geranium

When talking of Geranium we have four species: *G. maderense*, *G. canariense*, *G. rubescens* and *G. palmatum*. Of these *G. maderense* is another of the Tresco show stoppers. Over the first three or four years of its life it grows just foliage. Deeply toothed leaves up to 50cm (20in) long with red stalks form a large rosette. As the lower leaves die back they form a stem to hold up the plant itself. When the weather conditions dictate or the plant has attained a flowering size, from the centre of the plant will erupt numerous magenta flowers in a large headed panicle. Plants freely seed themselves about the garden in large numbers and can be easily transplanted.

Greyia sutherlandii

Grevillea

Another of the Proteaceae family to do well on Tresco. Grevillea are among the most popular plants for cultivation in their native country of Australia. Many flower constantly throughout the year with a range of flower colours such as red, yellow, orange and pink. Mostly small shrubs such as *Grevillea rosmarinifolia* and *G. sulphurea* do well on our upper terraces. On Tresco it is a very under used plant that will be given attention to build up our specie numbers.

Greyia

The well-named Natal bottlebrush is part of a genus of only three species. We grow two of them on Tresco. *Greyia sutherlandii* can form a small well-rounded tree with large leathery leaves. Large crimson flowers in clusters up to 15cm (6in) long form on the end of branches before full leaf development. Frost-tender the wood appears to be almost succulent when pruning.

Griselinia

Introduced to Tresco in 1857, this group of evergreen trees and shrubs stand up to the salt spray of the Atlantic gales with supreme ease. Used as hedge or single specimen they are grown for their foliage and have large glossy leathery leaves. They can tolerate full sun or shade conditions with equal measure.

Hakea

One species stands out when in flower in the winter months, *Hakea suaveolens*. It is widely planted around coastal areas with great success due to its flat, pointed sharp leaves. The creamy yellow globe-like flowers are sweetly scented and will last over a period of two months. Plants are easily grown from seed that is released in pairs from a small nut-like fruit.

Hardenbergia

Hardenbergia comptoniana makes a dramatic floral impact on the garden when in flower. Belonging to the family Fabaceae the climbing pea-like flowers from mauve to purplish blue shine out from its own foliage. It needs support of some sort or can be grown over a wall or bank. Plants can tolerate a wide range of soils and will take full sun but prefer shade at some point of the day. A white form does exist but is not as vigorous and therefore not so popular.

Hedychium gardnerianum

Hardenbergia comptoniana

Hakea suaveolens

Hedychium

A popular plant when sited in groups, Hedychium always look more tender than they really are. Grown for both foliage and wonderful exotic fragrant flowers. In the splendidly named family Zingberaceae they have stout, fleshy rhizomes. *Hedycium gardnerianum* from India flowers in July and August with fragrant yellow cylindrical racemes. Growing up to a height of 1.8m (6ft) means they are able to show well from backs of borders.

Hoheria

It is always a bonus when trees flower late in the season such as Hoheria. From New Zealand and both evergreen and deciduous the fragrant white flowers stand out against the lime green leaves. Very much a coastal tree, it can reach heights of up to 9m (30ft) making it a very fine specimen tree.

Homeria

A delicate South African corm this half-hardy group contain roughly thirty species. Scattered about our gravel paths live thousands of corms of *Homeria collina*. The delicate cup- shaped flower sits precariously on top of the slender stem. It can be very invasive but is not a major nuisance.

Hymenosporum

A one species genus introduced to Tresco in 1904 from Australia. An upright evergreen tree it will reach a height of at least 18m (60ft). Thin dark green leaves help this summer flowering tree show its creamy flowers. As the flowers age they turn to yellow and orange giving the appearance of a multi-coloured tree.

Iochroma

From the family Solanaceae these plants do very well positioned against south facing walls. From the forests of South America they are grown for the trumpet-like flowers that are typical of the group. *Iochroma cyanea* has very vivid deep purple flowers that hang in clusters. Very frost tender the foliage can be badly burnt causing die back. Very easy to propagate from cuttings.

Homeria collina (Frank Naylor)

Iochroma cyanea

Isoplexus sceptrum (Frank Naylor)

Isoplexus

Evergreen shrubs from the Canary Islands with only three species in the genus. All three grow on Tresco and do very well in our coastal climate. *Isoplexus sceptrum* is a woody, wide spreading shrub from Madeira. With us it flowers from April onwards, the large orange flowers on short stems sitting above the foliage. *Isoplexus* *canariensis* has an altogether more delicate flower. Will flower strongly even when growing in shady conditions.

Jubea

Palms play a large part in the Abbey Garden. As feature or spot plants they give so much to the garden visitor. *Jubea chilensis*, or, the Chilean wine palm has a large smooth barrel-like trunk and leaves up to 4.5m (15ft) long. Our single tree was planted in 1914 having now reached a height of some 9m (30ft).

Kunzea

As early as 1791 plants of Kunzea were introduced into cultivation from Australia. Most Kunzeas are shrubby and enjoy sandy soil. The leaf if crushed is strongly aromatic, as one would expect of a plant in the family Myrtaceae. *Kunzea baxteri* is by far the showiest of the genus, with large red bottlebrush flowers. It can flower quite early in the year in March/April.

Kunzea baxteri

Lampranthus

As rockery plants Lampranthus are hard to beat for sheer colour and impact. If garden visitors to Tresco had to pick a favourite plant then Lampranthus would top many lists. A frost-tender succulent it will survive drought to form large mats of foliage and flower. The species range is very wide and the seasonal flowering period can be from March to September. Daisy-like flowers sit above the foliage in hot bright colours that include white, red, orange, yellow, purple,

Jubea chilensis

pink and shades in between. The habit does vary among the species and forms from quite woody and upright to very prostrate and ground hugging. Plants grow easily from seed but if material is available then cuttings are more quickly convenient. Small 5 - 7.6cm (2 - 3in) cuttings should be taken after flowering. They will root very swiftly and can be planted as small plugs into walls and banks. Within twelve months a carpet of flower and foliage will have formed. Plants do need to be renewed as they lose vigour over four to five years. Species that stand out are *L. roseus*, *L. blandus*, *L. aureus* and *L. zeyheri*.

Lampranthus species

Lampranthus species

Lampranthus species (Frank Naylor)

Lapageria rosea (Frank Naylor)

Leucadendron argenteum (Jerry Harpur)

Leptospermum: three hybrids (Frank Naylor)

Leucadendron eucalyptifolium

Leucadendron species (Frank Naylor)

Lapageria

From the forests of Chile, this ever-green climber is grown for its showy bell-like flowers. Large waxy red trumpets up to 15cm(6in) long of *Lapageria rosea* clamber about the upper canopies of nearby trees.

Leptospermum

Mainly native of Australia they are cultivated for neat foliage and small compact flowers. Around eighty species of mainly large shrubs to small trees they do well in good soil conditions. *Leptospermum scoparium* seeds itself freely about our hillsides producing thickets of colour during the spring with flowers of white, pink and red. Very effective in a small garden and long lived.

Leucadendron

This group is very closely allied to *Protea* with highly coloured bracts rather than showy flowers. Needing the same growing conditions with low nutrient intake. Most are frost-tender and if planted in a protected spot the plants may sulk due to lack of air movement. The most prominent species has to be *Leucadendron argenteum*, the "Silver Tree". Covered in narrow silvery leaves our plants can withstand the full force of the Atlantic gales. The flowers are hidden in the foliage and are rarely seen.

Leucospermum cordifolium

Leucospermum

Still pushing along the *Proteaceae* theme comes the pincusion plant from South Africa. A low rounded shrub up to 1.2m (4ft) high with orange / red flowers. *Leucospermum cordifolium* opens its flowers in April and May.

Luma

A small genus with many name changes. The tree *Luma apiculata* is well known for its cinnamon bark colouring with the added bonus of late summer flowering. Clusters of white flowers up to 2.5cm (1in) flower well into October. Trees can reach up to15m (50ft) high. From Chile and Argentina they are frost hardy. If not kept in check natural seedlings can cause a problem.

Macropiper

A shade loving plant from New Zealand this evergreen shrub has shiny heart shaped leaves. Grown as a foliage plant it reaches up to 3m (10ft). Known as the pepper tree it also has a Maori name: "kawa-kawa". A variegated form *Macropiper excelsum variegatum* is also available.

Luma apiculata

Melaleuca

A genus of some two hundred and fifteen species from Australia and within the family Myrtaceae many of the species have several layers of paper-thin bark. Over many years this builds up and is then naturally shed by the tree. Significant numbers have bottle-brush type flowers very similar to the callistemon. In Australia Melaleuca is distributed over a wide range of habitats and climatic regions, from tropical to cool temperate and semi-arid desert to rainforest zones. Some species also occur in mountain ranges. Most species prefer acidic soils and species we grow which prefer these conditions include *M. squrrosa*, *M. squamea*, *M. ericifolia* and *M. nosophila*.

Meryta

A genus of twenty five small trees from the Pacific Islands we only grow one species here on Tresco, *Meryta sinclairii*. The leaves are very thick and leathery with a smooth upper surface and very large for a dicotyledon. They will stand out as feature plants growing to a height of up to 6m (20ft).

Metrosideros

If we had to choose one tree on Tresco above all others the metrosideros would be our choice. For tolerance to wind and salt spray it has no equal. As a specimen grown for flower, it is hard to match. We grow a range of species, including *M. diffusa* a climbing and scrambling plant, which flowers in April on rock faces with its typical brush-like scarlet red flowers. *M. robusta* will flower in May/June and is a tree that can actually begin its life as an epiphyte. *Metrosideros excelsa* is the most magnificent of all our species. Growing to epic size, up to 18m (60ft) high in a huge globe-like flower across the whole tree in July. Trees in flower can be seen from many miles away. It only has one drawback that we can see: intolerance to a hard frost. Once established however it has powers of recovery and will regenerate if damaged by cold conditions. Cuttings can be very easily taken after flowering from all species.

Metrosideros robusta

Ochagavia carnea (Frank Naylor)

Musschia woollastonii

Musschia

A plant often confused with *Echium pininiana* when in the foliage stage is *Musschia woollastonii* from Madeira. A large rosette of lanceolate leaves of up to 75cm (30in) long sit on a stem before producing a wonderful pyramid of creamy yellow flowers in either the second or third year. Will do well in both sun and shade. Generally it will not tolerate frost.

Ochagavia

A handsome Bromeliad from Chile this stemless and spiny-leafed plant forms large clumps up to 4.5m (15ft) across. In the summer months tubular, rose pink flowers are produced in the centre of spiny-toothed leaves. *Ochagavia carnea* has always attracted comment and is very similar to the Fascicularia also from Chile.

Oleaia X scilloniensis

Osteospermum "Tresco Purple"

Olearia

Widely used across the islands as a hedging plant this group is native of Australia and New Zealand. One species *Olearia traversii* is the mainstay where shelter is concerned, able to withstand the most ferocious of gales and highly tolerant of salt spray. Very quick growing it needs to be trimmed three or four times a year if grown as a hedge. Also grown as specimen plant it develops into a tree up to 9m (30ft) with splendidly branched trunks. An evergreen, leaves are a glossy dark green above with a white felt beneath. It can be cut down to ground level and will happily regenerate. *Olearia x Scilloniensis* (*O. lirata x O. phlogopappa*) is a natural hybrid that developed on Tresco in 1948. In the spring this shrub is covered with small white daisy-like flowers with a yellow centre.

Oscularia deltoides

Oscularia

Allied very closely to the Lampranthus or Mesembryanthemum is the group Oscularia. Plants are easily cultivated and are suitable for rockeries, embankments and particularly cliffs. Plants have spreading branches of succulent waxy leaves and form large spreading mats. *Oscularia deltoides* flowers in the spring to summer with small pink flowers. Cuttings can be rooted in pure sand.

Osteospermum

The family Compositae have always contributed a great deal in the range and volume of flower in the summer months about the garden. One plant that stands out is *Osteospermum*, a genus of subshrub perennials mainly from South Africa. Many cultivars have been chosen and named. One particular to Tresco is *Osteospermum* "Tresco Purple" or "Tresco Peggy", reputedly collected on a plant hunting trip from South Africa by Commander Tom Dorrien-Smith and named after his wife. It is a quick growing spreading plant with dark purple flowerheads up to 50mm (2in) across. Flowering almost non-stop through the year it is at its best from March to August. Others to lookout for are *O. ecklonis* (white) *O. jacundum* (mauve-purple) *O.*"Buttermilk"and *O.*"Whirligig".

Pelargonium

Tresco has an abundance of South African Pelargonium growing throughout the garden with many species and cultivars. Able to live outdoors all year it is unusual if they are lost to severe weather conditions. If plants are damaged then it is possible to cut down to ground level to promote regeneration from the roots. Scented leafed species such as *P. crispum* are planted on path edges to gain maximum effect when touched. *P. cucullatum* is a tall, shrubby plant that can grow to 1m (3ft) tall with large clusters of purple flowers. It does become woody and will need pruning. It does very well in full exposure with its tough leaves. *Pelargonium glutinosum* has sticky, glabrous leaves and will grow well in dry soils. *Pelargonium tomentosum* has naturalised on the hillsides and in the garden. It is highly scented with soft leaves and a peppermint scent. It has a scrambling habit with small pale pink and white flowers.

Pelargonium papillionaceum was collected only as recently as 1980. It died out in the snow freeze of 1987 but was replaced two years later. Growing to a height of 2.5m (8ft) it has the added bonus of large scented leaves and pink flowers.

Phoenix canariensis

Phoenix

From a genus with seventeen species Tresco Abbey Garden only grows one with any conviction, *Phoenix canariensis*, The Canary Island Date Palm. This tree dominates the garden and sets the tone for everything around it. One glance at our 12m (40ft) tall specimens confirms the thought that the garden is special within the British Isles. Introduced into the garden in 1894 they have steadily grown to a great maturity. With leaves up to 4.5m (15ft) long and bright yellow fruits, as a specimen tree they are unmissable to the garden visitor.

Pinus

Introduced to Tresco by T. A. Dorrien-Smith in 1874, *Pinus radiata* became the shelter tree for the gardens in the early years of its development. From Monterey, California it is well used to the force of Atlantic gales. It has three needles and large cones that will sit on the trees for up to twenty years. Our original plantings have reached up to 30m (100ft) high. As they mature there is a tendency to lose the lower branches and become top heavy. *Pinus pinea* the "Stone Pine" or "Umbrella Pine" from the Mediterranean has been planted in high numbers recently and will in years to come, we hope, dominate our skyline.

Puya chilensis

Protea cynaroides

Puya chilensis (Frank Naylor)

Protea

Unrivalled in beauty and variety Proteas represent one of the best-known plant families in South Africa. In Tresco Abbey Garden they have the same impact. The nutrient requirements of the Protea works perfectly in tandem with our soil, which is low in phosphates, and the floral reward is well worth waiting for. Without doubt the most visually spectacular of all the species grown in the garden is *Protea cynaroides* which is also the National flower of South Africa. Commonly known as the "King Protea" or sugarbush, due to the size of the flower. It is up to 30cm (12in) across with a goblet shaped flower of crimson red to pink and cream coloured bracts. Within the centre of the head sit hundreds of stamens that will gently open as the flower ages. *Protea neriifolia* is prominent about the garden and always performs with many flowers during most months of the year. In the bearded sugarbush group its flowers are always long lasting.

Protea compacta (Fiona Wilding)

Protea lepidocarpodendron

Puya

Natives of the Andes this wide ranging collection of *Bromeliads* live at high altitudes and are thus able to withstand both cold and drought conditions. Even gardeners are astounded at the architectural quality of both foliage and flower. Best known in the garden is *Puya chilensis*. It has foliage with hooked spines so vicious that gardeners refuse to weed amongst them. With a fast growing flower spike up to 2.5m (8ft) and a flower head covered in thick waxy yellow/green petals and pollen covered anthers, many local birds find the attraction too great. They emerge from nectar drinking competitions with pollen covered heads as if tropical birds. In the wild, humming birds would ordinarily pollinate, but on Tresco we welcome blackbirds and starlings to do the same work. Easy to propagate from seed.

Quercus

If the word oak is mentioned on Tresco it is to evergreen not deciduous that our thoughts will turn. One important aspect of the garden will always be shelter. *Quercus ilex,* the holm oak, native of S. W. Europe is used by us as a hedge plant. Grown to a height of 9m (30ft) our clipped hedges provide not just a wind-protecting barrier but serve as a major feature in the garden. The leaves are dark green and glossy and the hedge will produce acorns.

Rhopalostylis

The Nikau Palm from New Zealand, both north and south islands is at its best growing in the shady areas of the garden. It has a slender stem with long leaves up to 2.5m (8ft) long. A bright yellow flower will be followed by brighter red berries that will fall from the tree and freely seed. Young seedlings can be easily transplanted. We only grow the one species *Rhopalostylis sapida*.

Senecio

A large group of annuals, biannuals and perennials, Tresco is represented in more than one area. A popular 'weed' that seeds itself easily is *Senecio glastifolius*. Growing to 1m (3ft) high, the stem is topped by a multi headed flower in pink/purple. Freely seeding about the garden in great drifts. In the large shrub department, Senecio grandiflorus has very attractive large, soft leaves with big mops of yellow scented flowers.

Rhopalostylis sapida

Senecio grandiflorus

Senecio glastifolius

154

Sophora

An added bonus in the month of January is the flowering tree sophora from New Zealand. Trees can grow up to 9m (30ft) high and will freely grow from seed. An attractive leaf gives the appearance of an exotic but in fact Sophora will stand temperatures below freezing. The panicles of golden yellow flowers hang down in large clusters before the appearance of the foliage in March. For the smaller garden *Sophora* "Goldilocks" with a darker flower is available.

Sophora *"Goldilocks"*

Strelitzia

The Bird of Paradise plant from South Africa is always popular whether grown outdoors or as a pot plant. We grow three species on Tresco. Best known is *Strelitzia reginae*, the crane flower. Shrubby and clump forming the strong stem holds a humming bird like flower of orange and purple/blue. *Strelitzia nicolai* is more tree-like and can reach a height of 9m (30ft). It has a large predominantly white flower with blue tongue.

Strelitzia reginae

Sparmannia

A plant that stands out in the crowd is *Sparmannia africana* from Southern Africa. Known as African hemp it has large hairy, light green leaves up to 25cm (10in) long. Flowers are produced in the spring and summer. They are white with red reflex stamens that will open if touched. Leaves are liable to become ragged over a period of time. To refresh the plant heavy pruning will produce fresh leaves. Stems can grow as much as 3.5m (12ft) a year.

Sparmannia africana (Fiona Wilding)

Trachycarpus

Introduced into the Abbey Garden as early as 1854 this very hardy palm from Japan and China was planted as a group in an area known as the hop circle (hop plants were strung between the trunks of the palms). Single trunks although fairly slow growing will reach up to 9m (30ft) high. Small yellow flower-heads appear about the large fan-shaped leaves.

Watsonia *"Tresco Hybrid"* (Frank Naylor)

Yucca whipplei

Yucca

Related to the Agave, Yuccas are grown for their bold foliage as well as flower. Forming large open globe-like heads, they have long leaves often with sharp points. *Yucca whipplei* from the deserts of California will flower only periodically. When it does, the white flowered spike will grow up to 3.5m (12ft) high in just two weeks.

Watsonia

In the late summer months the gardens are ablaze with the flowers of *Watsonia* species and *Watsonia* "Tresco Hybrid". A plant from South Africa produced by a corm with evergreen sword shaped leaves and flower stems of predominantly orange and pink rising above the foliage. Large clumps will form over many years that will need splitting over a period of time.

BIBLIOGRAPHY

COCKAYNE L. 1928: 'Vegetation of New Zealand'.
Englemann, Leipzig.

ELLIOT W.R. & JONES D.L. 1980: 'Encyclopaedia of Australian
Plants'. Lothian, Sydney.

GILDERMEISTER H. 1995: 'Mediterranean Gardening, A Waterwise
Approach'. Moll, Spain.

HANBURY T. 1938: 'La Mortola Garden'.
Oxford University Press.

HUNKIN J.W. 1947: 'Journal of The Royal Horticultural Society'
Vol LXXII Part 5 / Part 6
Vol XCIII Part 8.

HUXLEY A. (Ed) 1992: 'The RHS Dictionary of Gardening'.
Macmillan, London.

INGLIS-JONES E. 1969: 'Augustus Smith of Scilly'.
Faber and Faber, London.

JONES L. 1994: 'Gardens of the French Riviera'.
Flammarion, Paris.

KING R. 1985: 'Tresco England's Island of Flowers'.
Constable, London.

LANCASTER R. and DE NOAILLES 1977: 'Mediterranean Plants and
Gardens'. Floraprint, Nottingham.

LATYMER H. 1990: 'The Mediterranean Gardener'.
Lincoln, London.

QUEST-RITSON C. 1992: 'The English Garden Abroad'.
Penguin, London.

PHILIPS R. & RIX M. 1997: 'Conservatory & Indoor Plants'.
Macmillan, London.

VAN WYK B.E.& GIDEON SMITH G. 1996: 'Guide to the Aloes of
South Africa'. Briza, South Africa.